THE USEFULNESS
OF THE USELESS

THE
USEFULNESS
OF THE
USELESS

Nuccio Ordine

Translated from the Italian
by Alastair McEwen

PAUL DRY BOOKS
Philadelphia 2017

First Paul Dry Books Edition, 2017

Paul Dry Books, Inc.
Philadelphia, Pennsylvania
www.pauldrybooks.com

The Usefulness of the Useless
L'Utilità Dell'Inutile
© Nuccio Ordine, 2013
© Bompiani – RCS Libri S.p.A., Milan 2013

Translation copyright © Alastair McEwen, 2017

Printed in the United States of America

CIP data available at the Library of Congress

ISBN-13: 978-1-58988-116-7

To Rosalia

CONTENTS

PART TWO

The University as Company, the Student as Client

PART THREE
Possession Kills:
Dignitas Hominis, **Love, Truth**

THE USEFULNESS
OF THE USELESS

INTRODUCTION

And the role of philosophy is precisely that of revealing to men the usefulness of the useless or, if you will, to teach them to distinguish between the two meanings of the word useful.

PIERRE HADOT, *Exercices spirituels et philosophie antique*

The oxymoron evoked by the title *The Usefulness of the Useless* deserves some explanation. The paradoxical usefulness of which I speak is not the usefulness in whose name humanistic learning—and, more generally, all learning that produces no profit—is considered useless. In a much more universal sense, I wished to place at the center of my reflections the idea of the usefulness of those forms of knowledge whose essential value is wholly free of any utilitarian end. Some knowledge is an end in itself that—precisely because of its free and selfless nature, far from any practical and commercial bond—can play a fundamental role in the cultivation of the spirit and in the civil and cultural development of humankind. Within this frame of reference, I consider *useful* everything that helps us become better.

But the logic of profit undermines those institutions (schools, universities, research centers, laboratories, museums, libraries, and archives) and those disciplines (classical and scientific) whose value ought to coincide with knowledge in itself, independently of the capacity to produce immediate gain or practical benefits. Of course, very often museums or archaeological sites can also be a source of extraordinary income. But their existence, contrary to what some would have us believe, cannot be subordinated to financial success: the life of a museum or of an archaeological site, like that of an archive or a library, is a treasure that the community must jealously safeguard at all costs.

This is why it is not true that in times of economic crisis anything goes. Just as, for the same reasons, it is not true that swings in the spread can justify the systematic destruction of all things considered useless with the juggernaut of inflexibility and linear cost cuts. These days Europe seems like a theater on whose stage it is mainly creditors and debtors who make a daily appearance. There is no political meeting or summit of high finance in which the obsession for accounts is not the sole item on the agenda. In a vortex that whirls in ever narrower circles, legitimate concerns over the repayment of debt are exacerbated to the point of causing effects diametrically opposite to those desired. The medicine of tough austerity, as various economists have noted, makes the patient inexorably weaker instead of curing him. Without wondering about the reasons why companies and countries have indebted themselves—rigor, oddly, does not even make a dent in rampant corruption and the fabulous salaries of ex-politicians, managers, bankers, and top-flight consultants—the many directors of this recessionary drift are in no way bothered by the fact that those who pay are above all the middle classes and the weakest members of society, millions of innocent human beings whose dignity has been expropriated.

It is not a question of foolishly evading responsibility for figures that don't add up. But neither is it possible to ignore the systematic destruction of any form of humanity and solidarity: banks and creditors ruthlessly claim, like Shylock in *The Merchant of Venice*, a pound of living flesh from those who cannot repay their debts. So, cruelly, many companies (which have enjoyed, for decades, the privatization of profits and the socialization of losses) fire workers, while governments suppress jobs, education, help for the disabled, and public health. "The right to have rights"—to quote from an important essay by Stefano Rodotà, whose title echoes an expression of Hannah Arendt's—is, in fact, subordinated to the dominance of the market, with the steadily growing risk of wiping out any form of respect for persons. By transforming people into goods and money, this perverse economic mechanism has given life to a monster, with no homeland and no pity, which will end up denying any form of hope to future generations, too.

Hypocritical efforts to avert Greece's leaving the European community—but the same reflections could hold for Italy or Spain—are the fruit of a cynical calculation (the price to pay would be even greater than that caused by the failure to repay the debt itself) and not of a genuine political culture founded on the idea that a Europe without Greece would be inconceivable, because the ancient roots of western knowledge are sunk deeply in the Greek language and civilization. Are debts contracted with the banks and high finance powerful enough to wipe the slate clean at a stroke and cancel the most *important* debts that, over the centuries, we have contracted with those who made us the gift of an extraordinary artistic and literary, musical and philosophical, scientific and architectural heritage?

In this brutal context, the usefulness of useless knowledge is radically opposed to the dominant usefulness that, in the name of exclusively economic interest, is steadily killing the memory of the past, the classical disciplines and languages, education, free research, imagination, art, critical thinking, and the civil horizon that ought to inspire all human activity. In the universe of utilitarianism, a hammer is worth more than a symphony, a knife more than a poem, and a monkey wrench more than a painting: because it is easy to understand the efficacy of a tool while it is ever more difficult to understand the utility of music, literature, or art.

Rousseau once remarked that the "ancient politicians talked incessantly about customs and virtues; ours talk only about trade and money." Those things that do not produce profit are considered to be a superfluous luxury, a dangerous obstacle. "All that is not useful is to be disdained," Diderot observed, because "time is too precious to waste in idle speculation."

It suffices to read the splendid verses of Charles Baudelaire to grasp the disquiet of the poet-albatross, a gigantic master of the skies who, once he has descended among men, is mocked by a public drawn by very different interests ("How clumsy and gawky this winged traveler is!/Once so beautiful, how droll he is, how ugly!/One man pokes at his beak with his pipe,/Another limps in mocking imitation of the cripple that flew!"). And not without ironic desolation, in his *Dictionary of Received Ideas* Flaubert defines poetry as "wholly useless" because "out of fashion" and poet as a "synonym for fool" and "dreamer." Not even the sublime final verse of a lyric poem by Hölderlin, in which he highlights the poet's fundamental role, seems to have any value: "What remains, however, is what the poets create."

The following pages do not claim to form an organic text. They reflect the fragmentariness that inspired them. All I wanted to do was to collect, in an open container, quotations and thoughts accumulated over many years of teaching and research. I did this in total freedom, without any constraints and with the awareness that I had merely sketched in an incomplete and partial portrait. And as often happens in collections and anthologies, the absences end up being more significant than the presences. Aware of these limitations, I have subdivided this essay into three parts: the first is devoted to the theme of the useful uselessness of literature; the second is on the disastrous effects caused by the logic of profit in the fields of teaching, research, and cultural activities in general; in the third part, with the aid of a few revealing examples, I have re-interpreted some classics that, over the centuries, have shown the illusory impact of possession and its devastating effects on people's dignity, on love, and on truth.

I have added to my brief reflections an excellent (and, alas, little known) essay written by Abraham Flexner in 1937 and republished in 1939 with some additions. Among the authoritative founders of the Institute for Advanced Study in Princeton—established with the precise aim of encouraging inquiry free of any utilitarian constraints and inspired exclusively by the curiosity of its illustrious members, among whom I should mention at least Albert Einstein and Robert Oppenheimer—Flexner, a celebrated American scientist and pedagogue, presents us with a fascinating account of the story of some great discoveries to show how theoretical scientific research considered to be absolutely useless, because devoid of any practical purpose, unexpectedly favored applications, from telecommunications to electricity, which were later revealed to be of fundamental importance to humanity.

Flexner's point of view struck me as being very efficacious in clearing the field of all confusion: creating contrapositions between classical and scientific learning—as has happened several times since the 1950s, after the renowned essay by C. P. Snow—would have inevitably caused the debate to slide into the quicksands of sterile polemic. And, above all, it would have confirmed a total disinterest in the necessary unity of knowledge—in that indispensable *nouvelle alliance*, about which the Nobel Laureate Ilya Prigogine has written some illuminating pages—unfortunately today ever more threatened by the parceling out and ultra-specialization of knowledge. Flexner shows us brilliantly how science has much to teach us about the usefulness of the useless. And how, together with humanists, scientists have also played, and still do, a most important role in the battle against the dictatorship of profit, to defend the liberty and the gratuitousness of knowledge and research.

In addition, awareness of the difference between purely speculative, disinterested science and applied science was widespread among the ancients, as is borne out by Aristotle's reflections and also by some anecdotes attributed to great scientists of the caliber of Euclid and Archimedes.

But such fascinating matters might lead us too far from the point. Now it is important for me to underline the vital importance of those values that we cannot *weigh* and *measure* with instruments calibrated to assess *quantitas* and not *qualitas*. And, at the same time, I wish to make a claim for the fundamental nature of those *investments* that do not produce immediate returns and cannot be turned into cash.

In itself, knowledge acts as a hindrance to the delusion of omnipotence of money and utilitarianism. True, everything can be bought. From legislators to judges, from power to success: everything has its price. But not knowledge: the price to be paid for knowing is of a completely different kind. Not even a blank check would allow us to acquire mechanically what is the exclusive fruit of an individual effort and an inexhaustible passion. No one, in short, can tread the laborious path to learning in our stead. Without great inner motivation, the most prestigious degree bought with money will bring no real knowledge and will not favor any genuine metamorphosis of the spirit.

Socrates once explained this to Agathon, when in the *Symposium* he challenges the idea that knowledge can be transmitted mechanically from one human being to the other like water that runs along a thread from a full container to an empty one:

> It would be really fine, Agathon, if knowledge were able to flow from the fullest to the emptiest among us and all we had to do was to be in contact one with the other, like the water that flows along a woolen thread from the fuller goblet to the emptier one.

But there's more. Only knowledge is still able to challenge the laws of the market. I can share my knowledge with others without impoverishing myself. I can teach a student the theory of relativity or read together with her a page of Montaigne thereby giving rise to a miraculous virtuous circle in which both the giver and the receiver are enriched at the same time.

Of course it is not easy to understand, in our world dominated by *homo economicus*, the usefulness of the useless and, above all, the uselessness of the useful (how many unnecessary consumer goods are sold to us as indispensable?). It hurts to see human beings, unaware of the growing desertification that smothers the spirit, devoted exclusively to amassing money and power. It hurts to see the triumph on television and in the media of new portrayals of success, in the form of the entrepreneur who manages to create an empire through fraud, or of the rogue politician who humiliates parliament by voting for *ad personam* legislation. It hurts to see men and women in a mad dash toward the promised land of gain, where all that surrounds them—nature, objects, other human beings—arouses no interest. The gaze fixed on the objective to be attained makes it impossible to grasp the joy of little everyday gestures and to discover the beauty that pulses through our lives: in a sunset, in a starry sky, in the tenderness of a kiss, in a flower that blooms, in the flight of a butterfly, and in a child's smile. Because, often, greatness is perceived better in the simplest things.

"If one cannot understand the usefulness of the useless, and the uselessness of the useful, one cannot understand art," Eugène Ionesco justly observed. And it is no accident that, many years before Ionesco, Kakuzo Okakura, in describing the tea ritual, identified the pleasure of picking a flower to give to a lady friend as the precise moment in which the human species rose above the animals. Man "entered the realm of art," the Japanese writer said in *The Book of Tea*, "when he perceived the subtle use of the useless." At one and the same time, a double luxury: the flower (the object) and the act of plucking it (the gesture) both represent the useless, thus calling into question both the necessary and profit.

True poets know well that only far from calculation and haste is it possible to cultivate poetry: "Being an artist," says Rainer Maria Rilke in a passage from *Let-*

ters to a Young Poet, "means, not reckoning and count-
ing, but ripening like the tree which does not force its
sap and stands confident in the storms of spring without fear that after them may come no summer." Poetry
does not bow to the logic of haste and the useful. In
fact, at times, as Edmond Rostand's Cyrano suggests
in the final lines of the play, the useless is necessary to
make all things more beautiful: "What's that you say? It
is *useless*? But no one fights in hope of success! No! No,
it is far better to fight when it is *useless*."

We need the useless the way we need our vital func-
tions in order to live. "Poetry," Ionesco reminds us, "the
need to imagine and create, is as fundamental as the
need to breathe. To breathe is to live and not to escape
from life." It is this very breath, as Pietro Barcellona
pointed out, that comes to express the "surplus of life
with respect to life itself," becoming "energy that circulates invisibly and goes beyond life, even though it
is immanent in life." It is in the depths of those activities thought to be superfluous, in fact, that we can per-
ceive the stimulus to think of a better world, to cultivate
the utopia of being able to attenuate, if not to wipe out,
the widespread injustices and the distressing inequalities that weigh (or ought to weigh) heavily on our conscience. Especially when there is an economic crisis,
when the temptations of utilitarianism and the wick-
edest egoism seem to be the only star and the only life-
line, we need to understand that it is precisely those
activities deemed useless that could help us escape from
prison, save us from asphyxia, transform a dull life, a

non-life, into a fluid and dynamic one, oriented toward a *curiositas* for the spirit and human affairs.

While the biophysicist and philosopher Pierre Lecomte du Noüy invited us to reflect on the fact that "in the scale of beings, only man performs useless acts," two psychotherapists (Miguel Benasayag and Gérard Schmit) suggest that "the usefulness of the useless is the usefulness of life, of creation, of love and desire," because "the useless produces that which is most useful to us, which is created without shortcuts, without saving time, over and above the mirage created by society." This explains why Mario Vargas Llosa, on receiving the Nobel Prize in 2010, rightly pointed out that "a world without literature would be a world without desires or ideals or irreverence, a world of automatons deprived of what makes the human being really human: the capacity to move out of oneself and into another, into others, modeled with the clay of our dreams."

And who can say if, through the words of Mrs. Erlynne—"In modern life margin is everything"—Oscar Wilde did not wish to allude to the *superfluity* of his own profession as a writer (perhaps thinking of a famous line by Voltaire, "le superflu, chose très necéssaire" ["the superfluous, a very necessary thing"]).* With that "margin" or excess—far from connoting, negatively, a

*Translator's note: Here, "margin" should be understood as that which is more than absolutely necessary, and hence connotative of *superfluous*. The Italian translation of Wilde has "superfluo" for margin.

"surplus" or something "superabundant"—he intends, instead, that which exceeds the necessary, which is not indispensable, which goes beyond the essential. Hence, that which comes to coincide with the vital idea of a flux that flows and constantly renews itself and also with the notion of uselessness—as he had already hinted some years before in the preface to *The Picture of Dorian Gray*: "All art is quite useless."

If we think about it, though, a work of art does not ask to come into the world. Or to borrow another splendid observation by Ionesco, the work of art "asks to be born" in the same way "as a child asks to be born": "A child is not born for society's sake," the dramatist explains, "although society claims him. He is born for the sake of being born. A work of art too is born for the sake of being born, it imposes itself on its author, it demands existence without asking or considering whether society has called for it or not." This does not change the fact that society can "claim the work of art": and also while it can "use it as it likes," or "condemn it" or "destroy it," the fact remains that "a work of art may or may not fulfill a social function, but it is not equivalent to this social function." And while "it is absolutely necessary that art . . . should have a purpose," Ionesco concludes, "I shall say it ought to remind people that there are some activities which serve no useful purpose and that it is imperative such things should be."

Without this awareness, it would be difficult to understand a historical paradox: when barbarism gets the upper hand, the deep hatred of the fanatic turns against not only human beings but also against libraries and works of art, against monuments and great masterpieces. The destructive fury falls on those held to be useless: the sacking of the royal library in Luoyang by the hand of the Xiongnu in China, the burning of the pagan manuscripts in Alexandria decreed by the intolerance of bishop Theophilus, the heretical books put to the torch by the Inquisition, the *seditious* works burned by the Nazis in Berlin, the splendid Buddhas of Bamiyan razed to the ground by the Taliban in Afghanistan, or the manuscripts of the Sahel and the statues of Al Farouk in Timbuktu threatened by the jihadis. Useless and harmless things, silent and inoffensive, but perceived as a danger for the mere fact of existing.

Amid the rubble of a Europe destroyed by the blind violence of war, Benedetto Croce identified the signs of the coming of the new barbarians, capable of pulverizing in a single moment the long history of a great civilization:

> When barbarian vigor [grows strong again] not only do they overwhelm and oppress those who represent [civilization], but they turn to demolishing their works, which for them were instruments of other works, and they destroy monuments of beauty, systems of thought, all the evidence of the noble past, closing schools, dispersing or burning museums and libraries and archives . . . There is no need to seek examples of this in remote history, because the story of our own day offers such a copious number of them that even our horror at this has been dulled.

But also those who erect walls, as Jorge Luis Borges reminds us, can easily have books burned, because in both cases you end up "burning the past":

> I read, some days past, that the man who ordered the erection of the almost infinite wall of China was that first emperor, Shih Huang-Ti, who also decreed that all books prior to him be burned. That these two vast operations—the five to six hundred leagues of stone opposing the barbarians, the rigorous abolition of history, that is, of the past—should originate in one person and be in some way his attributes inexplicably satisfied and, at the same time, disturbed me.

The sublime disappears when humanity, having been plunged down into the lower part of Fortune's wheel, touches bottom. Man becomes ever poorer even as he thinks he is enriching himself: "if, at every turn, you deceive and defraud, solicit and make deals," Cicero warns in the *Stoic Paradoxes*, "if you steal and take things with violence, if you rob your partners, if you despoil the treasury . . . then, tell me: do these practices point to a man with a very great abundance of goods or one who has absolutely none of them?"

It is no accident that in the closing pages of the treatise *On the Sublime*, one of the most important ancient works of literary criticism that has come down to us, pseudo-Longinus clearly identifies the causes that produced the decline of eloquence and knowledge in Rome, and ensured that no great writers came along after the end of the republican regime: "the desire for riches, for which we are all insatiably ill [is leading us] to slavery . . . The love of money is a sickness that shrivels the soul." By following these false idols, the selfish man "no longer looks upward" and ends up desiccating "spiritual greatness." Amid this moral decay, "when corruption is the arbiter of all our lives," there is no room for any type of sublime. But the sublime, pseudo-Longinus reminds us again, also needs liberty: "Liberty, it is said, is that which suffices to nourish the sentiments of great spirits, and to give them hope."

Giordano Bruno also attributes the love of money with the destruction of knowledge and the essential values on which civil life is founded: "Wisdom and justice" he writes in *De immenso*, "began to abandon the world when the learned, organized into sects, started to use their doctrine to make money . . . Both religion and philosophy are vanquished by such attitudes; states, kingdoms, and empires are overturned, ruined, and outlawed together with sages, princes, and peoples."

Even John Maynard Keynes, the father of macroeconomics, revealed in a lecture in 1928, that "the gods" on which economic life is founded are inevitably spirits of evil. Of a *necessary* evil that for "at least another hundred years" would have obliged us to "pretend to ourselves and to everyone that fair is foul, and foul is fair; for foul is useful and fair is not." Humankind, in short, would have had to continue (until 2028!) to consider "avarice and usury and precaution" as indispensable vices for leading us "out of the tunnel of economic necessity into daylight." And only then, widespread prosperity having been attained, would our grandchildren (the title of the lecture, "Economic Possibilities for our

Grandchildren," is most eloquent) finally be able to understand that the good is always better than the useful:

> I see us free, therefore, to return to some of the most sure and certain principles of religion and traditional virtue—that avarice is a vice, that the exaction of usury is a misdemeanor, and the love of money is detestable, that those walk most truly in the paths of virtue and sane wisdom who take least thought for the morrow. We shall once more value ends above means and prefer the good to the useful. We shall honor those who can teach us how to pluck the hour and the day virtuously and well, the delightful people who are capable of taking direct enjoyment in things, the lilies of the field who toil not, neither do they spin.

Even though Keynes's prophecy did not come true—to this day the prevalent economics, unfortunately, persists in looking only at production and consumption and holding in contempt all that does not serve the utilitarian logic of the market and, therefore, continues to sacrifice the "arts of joy" to profit—his sincere conviction is still precious for us: the genuine essence of life coincides with the good (namely that which the commercial democracies have always considered useless) and not with the useful.

About ten years later, from a very different angle, Georges Bataille also wondered, in *The Limit of the Useful*, about the need to conceive an economics with an eye to anti-utilitarianism. Unlike Keynes, Bataille had no illusions about the presumed *noble purposes* of utilitarian processes, because "capitalism clearly has nothing in common with any concerns about improving the human condition." Only apparently does it seem to have "as its end the improvement of the standard of living," but this is a "deceptive perspective." In point of fact, "modern industrial production raises average standards without mitigating the inequalities between the classes and, all things considered, remedies social unrest only incidentally." In this context, only *surplus*—when it is not used "in relation to productivity"—can be linked to "the finest art, poetry, and the full blossoming of human life." Without this *surplus* energy, far from the accumulation and growth of wealth, it would be impossible to free life of "servile considerations that dominate a world devoted to increased production."

Yet George Steiner—a great champion of the classics and the humanist values "that privilege the life of the mind"—has said that, at the same time, in a dramatic manner "high culture and enlightened decency offered no protection against totalitarian barbarism." Many times, alas, we have seen thinkers and artists show indifference to brutal decisions or, even, become the moral *accomplices* of dictators and regimes that put such decisions into practice. It's true. This grave problem raised by Steiner makes me think of the stupendous dialogue between Marco Polo and Kublai Khan that ends Italo Calvino's *Invisible Cities*. Pressed by the sovereign's concerns, the indefatigable traveler offers us a dramatic fresco of the inferno around us:

> The inferno of the living is not something that will be; if there is one, it is what is already here, the inferno

where we live every day, that we form by being together. There are two ways to escape suffering it. The first is easy for many: accept the inferno and become such a part of it that you can no longer see it. The second is risky and demands constant vigilance and apprehension: seek and learn to recognize who and what, in the midst of the inferno, are not inferno, and make them endure, give them space.

But what can help us to understand, amid the inferno, that which is not inferno? It is difficult to give an absolute answer to this question. Calvino himself, in his essay "Why Read the Classics?" while recognizing that the "classics help us understand who we are and the point we have reached," cautions us against thinking that "the classics must be read because they serve some purpose." At the same time, though, Calvino maintains that "reading the classics is always better than not reading them."

"Culture, like love," Rob Riemen rightly observes, "does not possess a capacity to compel. It offers no guarantees. And yet, the only chance of attaining and protecting our human dignity is offered to us by culture, by liberal education." This is why I believe that, in any case, it is *better* to carry on the fight and to believe that the classics and education, that the cultivation of the superfluous and of things that do not produce profit, can in any event help us to *resist*, to keep the torch of hope alight, and to glimpse that ray of light that allows us to walk a dignified path.

Among the many uncertainties, however, one thing is certain: if we allow the gratuitous to die, if we give up the generative power of the useless, if we listen only to this deadly siren song that drives us to chase after profit, all we shall be able to do is produce a society that is sick and devoid of memory which, disoriented, will end up losing the sense of itself and of life. And then, when the desertification of the spirit has made us insensible, it will be really hard to imagine that the foolish *homo sapiens* can still play a role in making humanity more human . . .

NOTE

This essay, which marks the convergence of a series of scattered reflections, has its origins in various speeches I have given over the last ten years, including the lecture given on April 2012 at the Universidade Federal do Rio Grande do Sul in Porto Alegre, on the occasion of my receiving an honorary degree. I should like to thank my friend Irving Lavin, of the Princeton Institute for Advanced Study, for having brought to my attention the essay by Abraham Flexner. In June 2011, during a round table held in Naples at the Istituto Italiano per gli Studi Filosofici, struck by the title of my speech *The Useful Uselessness of the Humanistic Disciplines*, Lavin gave me Flexner's essay, which I did not know at the time. This work is indebted to some unforgettable and intense useless conversations with George Steiner and Alain Segonds. Without my students at the University of Calabria and at the various foreign universities in which I have taught over these years I likely would not have understood many aspects of the usefulness of the useless. Gerardo Marotta, president of the Istituto Italiano per gli Studi Filosofici, has devoted his entire life to the defense of the classics and culture.

I am immensely grateful to Jürgen Renn, director of the Max-Planck-Institut für Wissenschaftsgeschichte in Berlin and to the colleagues there with whom I discussed the themes developed in this book, when I was visiting scholar in 2013.

I thank my editors (Oliviero Toscani and Silvia Trabattoni) and the young colleagues who carefully reviewed the drafts (Marco Dondero, Maria Cristina Figorilli, and Zaira Sorrenti). My heartfelt thanks also to Elisabetta Sgarbi, Mario Andreose, and Eugenio Lio for their valuable suggestions and for having wished to accept my work.

PART ONE

The Useful Uselessness of Literature

And this was indeed Gavroche's home.
O unforeseen usefulness of the useless!
VICTOR HUGO, *Les Misérables*

1. "He who acquires not, exists not"

In an autobiographical account, Vincenzo Padula (1819–93), a revolutionary priest from Calabria, recalls the first lesson in life he learned at home, when he was still a young student. After giving his father an unsatisfactory reply to an insidious question ("How is it that in the alphabet of every language the *A* comes first and the *E* after it?"), the seminarian listened with lively curiosity to his father's explanation: "In this wretched world he who a*cquires*, e*xists*, and he who a*cquires* not, e*xists* not," which is why the letter *a* always comes before the letter *e*. But there's more: in civil society the have-nots constitute the bulk of the *consonants*, "because they are *consonant* with the *voice* of the rich man, and conform to the *vowel*, without which I defy you to show how the consonant could have a sound."

Almost two centuries later, the image of a dichotomous society rigidly divided into masters and servants, into wealthy exploiters and poor folks reduced to the level of brute beasts, as Padula described it, almost no longer corresponds to the portrait of the world we live in. There remains, however, in very different and more sophisticated forms, a supremacy of *having* over *being*, a dictatorship of profit and possession, which dominates all fields of knowledge and all our everyday behaviors. *Appearing* counts for more than does *being*: that which can be flaunted—a luxury automobile or a designer watch, a prestigious job or a position of power—has far more value than a person's culture or level of education.

2. Knowledge without profit is useless!

It is no accident that in the last few decades the humanities have come to be considered useless, and that they are marginalized not only in scholastic programs, but above all in state budgets and the resources of private bodies and foundations. Why put money into an area that will produce no profit? Why earmark funds for areas of knowledge that do not bring in a fast, tangible economic return?

Within this context founded exclusively on the need to weigh and measure on the basis of criteria that favor *quantitas*, literature (but the same argument could hold for other humanistic studies and for those forms of scientific knowledge that have no immediate utilitarian purpose) can take on a fundamental and most important function: its very immunity to any aspiration to make profit could set it up, per se, as a form of resistance to the selfishness of the present, as an antidote to the barbarism of profit that has gone so far as to corrupt our social relations and our most intimate affections. Its very existence, in fact, draws the attention to *gratuitous-*

ness and *selflessness*, values these days considered to be unconventional and out of fashion.

3. What's water? An anecdote from David Foster Wallace

Here's why at the beginning of every academic year I like to read to my students a passage from a speech given by David Foster Wallace to graduating students at Kenyon College.

On 21 May 2005, Wallace—who died tragically in 2008, at age forty-six—told a little story that wonderfully illustrates the role and function of culture:

> There are these two young fish swimming along, and they happen to meet an older fish swimming the other way, who nods at them and says, "Morning, boys, how's the water?" And the two young fish swim on for a bit, and then eventually one of them looks over at the other and goes, "What the hell is water?"

The author himself provides us with the key to his account: "The immediate point of the fish story is that the most obvious, ubiquitous, important realities are often the ones that are the hardest to see and talk about." Like the two young fish, we don't realize the true nature of the *water* in which we spend every minute of our lives. We are unaware, in fact, that literature and the humanities, that culture and education constitute the ideal amniotic fluid in which the ideas of democracy, freedom, justice, secularity, equality, the right

to criticize, tolerance, solidarity, and the common good
can enjoy vigorous development.

4. Colonel Buendía's little gold fish

Allow me to consider for a moment a novel that stirred
the dreams of generations of readers. I am thinking of *One Hundred Years of Solitude* by Gabriel García Márquez. Perhaps in the rational folly of Aureliano
Buendía it is possible to find the useless fecundity of literature. Closed up in his secret laboratory, the revolutionary colonel makes little gold fish in exchange for
gold coins that he then melts down to make more gold
fish. This vicious circle does not escape the criticism of
Ursula, the fond mother worried about her son's future:

> With her terrible practical sense she could not under-
> stand the colonel's business as he exchanged little fishes
> for gold coins and then converted the coins into little
> fishes, and so on, with the result that he had to work
> all the harder with the more he sold in order to satisfy
> an exasperating vicious circle. Actually, what interested
> him was not the business but the work.

Moreover, the colonel himself confesses that his "only
happy moments, since that remote afternoon when his
father had taken him to see ice, had taken place in his
silver workshop where he passed the time putting little
gold fishes together":

> He had had to start thirty-two wars and had had to
> violate all of his pacts with death and wallow like a hog

in the dung heap of glory in order to discover the privileges of simplicity almost forty years late.

Probably, it is this very simplicity, inspired only by genuine joy and far from any ambition to make a profit, which is the foundation of the creative act that gives life to what we call literature. A gratuitous act, devoid of any precise aim and one capable of eluding any commercial logic. Useless, therefore, because it cannot be turned into money. But necessary in order to express with its own existence a value alternative to the supremacy of the laws of the market and profit.

5. Dante and Petrarch: literature should not be subservient to profit

Some founding fathers of Western literature also expressed their opinion on these themes. To cite one illustrious example, in the *Convivio* (The Banquet), Dante condemns those pseudo-literati who do not "acquire learning for its own sake" but only to make it subservient to profit:

> And, to their dishonor, I say that they should not be considered as men of letters, since they do not acquire learning for its own sake but only to gain money or honors; just as we would not consider someone a lyre player if he kept a lyre in order to hire it out, instead of playing it.

Learning, in short, has nothing to with utilitarian and low purposes connected with the accumulation of money. And it is to this disinterested love of knowledge that Petrarch devotes a series of reflections in prose and in verse with the intention to show his scorn for a lost "crowd" that lives exclusively to amass wealth ("Poor and naked go you, Philosophy,/Says the crowd bent on contemptible gain"). In this famous sonnet from the *Canzoniere*, the poet encourages an illustrious friend not to give up the "lofty enterprise" of composing works, even though the great effort can only be rewarded, at best, with the noble glory of myrtle and laurel:

> Greed and sleep and idle beds
> Have cast out all virtue from the world
> And so our nature, vanquished by this,
> Has all but lost its way;
> And every kindly light of heaven
> Which informs human life is grown so feeble
> That if one says a river flows down from
> Helicon it is hailed as a wondrous thing.
>
> What longing for myrtle, and for laurel?
> Poor and naked go you, Philosophy,
> Says the crowd bent on contemptible gain.
> Few fellows shall you have on the other road,
> And so I beg you all the more, gentle spirit:
> Do not forsake your lofty enterprise.

6. The literature of utopia and golden chamber pots

A similar disdain for money, gold, silver, and all activities whose purpose is profit and trade is found in Renaissance literature on utopia. On the famous islands, located in mysterious places far from Western civilization, all forms of individual property are condemned in the name of the collective interest. The rapacity of individuals is opposed by a model based on love of the common good. Apart from the undeniable differences between these texts and the objective limits of certain aspects of the social organization they propose, what emerges clearly is the severe criticism of a contemporary reality dominated by a contempt for social justice and learning. Through the literature of utopia, authors show the defects and contradictions of a European society that has lost the essential values of human life and solidarity.

In Thomas More's seminal work, *Utopia* (1516), the islanders detest gold so much that they use it to make chamber pots:

> They eat and drink out of vessels of earth or glass, which make an agreeable appearance, though formed of brittle materials; while they make their chamber-pots and close-stools of gold and silver, and that not only in their public halls but in their private houses. Of the same metals they likewise make chains and fetters for their slaves, to some of which, as a badge of infamy, they hang an earring of gold, and make others wear a chain or a coronet of the same metal; and thus they take care by all possible means to render gold and silver of no esteem . . .

For the Utopians, in fact, where "there is private property . . . money is the standard of all things," thus making it impossible to do things justly and in favor of the state:

Though, to speak plainly my real sentiments, I must freely own that as long as there is any property, and while money is the standard of all other things, I cannot think that a nation can be governed either justly or happily: not justly, because the best things will fall to the share of the worst men; nor happily, because all things will be divided among a few (and even these are not in all respects happy), the rest being left to be absolutely miserable.

In the same way, in *The City of the Sun* (1623), by Tommaso Campanella, the Solarians see in property and the desire to possess things the principal causes of corruption, which drive man to grasp at the property of the state:

> They say that all private property is acquired and improved for the reason that each one of us has his own home and wife and children. From this, self-love springs. For when we raise a son to riches and dignities, and leave an heir too much wealth, we become . . . ready to grasp at the property of the State.

Campanella, who puts learning at the center of his *civitas*, is convinced that "wealth [makes men] insolent, proud, ignorant, traitors, assumers of what they know not." The Solarians—unlike the Spanish who "sought new regions for the lust for gold and riches"—travel only to acquire new knowledge.

Even Francis Bacon—who has a place all of his own in utopian literature, and not only because property is not banned in his *New Atlantis* (1627)—nonetheless felt it important to emphasize that his islanders do not trade for "gold, silver, or jewels; nor for silks; nor for spices; nor any other commodity" but only to increase knowledge, to be informed about the "inventions of all the world" and to procure books "in every kind." And although the elitist principles that inspire the house of Solomon are based on enlightened progress, on practical knowledge and technology connected with humanity's needs, Bacon's project, as Raymond Trousson suggests, "is not economic in nature" but is based especially on the "needs of modern science."

Pursuing well-being and allowing the circulation of gold and silver also means dealing with the ambiguities of technology and the perils of corruption. On this island, in fact, the functionaries consider themselves loyal servants of the state and the common good. And their ethical code prevents them from accepting gifts of money, as the foreigners who chance to land in Bensalem tell us with amazement:

> So he left us; and when we offered him some pistolets, he smiling said, "He must not be twice paid for one labour": meaning (as I take it) that he had salary sufficient of the State for his service. For (as I after learned) they call an officer that taketh rewards, "twice paid."

7. Jim Hawkins: treasure hunter or numismatist?

But fabled islands were not just models of society in which wealth and injustice are held in contempt. Robert Louis Stevenson, in one of the most famous adventure stories of all time, created a legendary place where tales of pirates and murder are interwoven with vast fortunes. In *Treasure Island*, in fact, the entire story hinges on the troubled voyage of the *Hispaniola* to recover the fabulous booty buried by Captain Flint in an obscure atoll in the Caribbean:

> How many it had cost in the amassing, what blood and sorrow, what good ships scuttled on the deep, what brave men walking the plank blindfold, what shot of cannon, what shame and lies and cruelty, perhaps no man alive could tell.

In the excited dialogue with doctor Livesey, squire Trelawney not only fails to hide his admiration for the buccaneer Flint ("The Spaniards were so prodigiously afraid of him, that, I tell you, sir, I was sometimes proud he was an Englishman"), but he also immediately forms a company to fit out a ship and set sail in order to win the huge sums of money illegally amassed by the pirates. This enterprise, as Geminello Alvi suggests, reveals at the same time the "duplicity of the two gentlemen" and the "relationship between the piracy industry and the capitalist." So the new *conquistadores*, ready to take possession of the legendary Flint's ill-gotten gains, hasten to seize their chance:

> "Money!" cried the squire. "Have you heard the story? What were these villains after but money? What do they care for but money? For what would they risk their rascal carcasses but money?"

Young Jim Hawkins, the protagonist of the story, takes ship with his *partners*. And after having overcome various trials and tribulations and having risked his life several times, the boy finally reaches the cave where the colossal pile of loot is hidden. But here the reader gets a surprise: when he comes into possession of the fortune amassed by the unscrupulous corsairs, Jim starts to pack up the treasure to transport it to the ship, showing complete indifference to the material value of the coins:

> It was a strange collection, like Billy Bones's hoard for the diversity of coinage, but so much larger and so much more varied that I think I never had more pleasure than in sorting them. English, French, Spanish, Portuguese, Georges and Louises, doubloons and double guineas and moidores and sequins, the pictures of all the kings of Europe for the last hundred years, strange Oriental pieces stamped with what looked like wisps of string or bits of spider's web, round pieces and square pieces, and pieces bored through the middle, as if to wear them round your neck—nearly every variety of money in the world must, I think, have found a place in that collection; and for number, I am sure they were like autumn leaves, so that my back ached with stooping and my fingers with sorting them out.

After a difficult initiatory experience in which Jim learns above all to recognize the diverse faces of evil, he looks at those gold and silver pieces with all the wonder of the junior numismatist, without feeling any attraction for their purchasing power. Unlike the grasping members of the crew, he has fun classifying the coins, fascinated by the variety of the faces of the sovereigns portrayed and the strangeness of the engraved designs. As if their value, devoid of any economic interest, were limited exclusively to the historical-artistic sphere. All that risk only to discover, at the end of the adventure, that the real treasure does not coincide with the doubloons and the sequins but with the culture of which they are the expression. Thus—in line with Stevenson's conviction, made explicit elsewhere, that *being* counts for more than *having*—in the mysterious Caribbean atoll, Jim understands, thanks to a useless *curiositas*, that those engravings are worth far more than their venal quotation because, apart from exhibiting various expressions of beauty, they also document memorable moments in the affairs of peoples and kingdoms. By now immune to gold fever, in the closing lines he confesses he has no regrets regarding the ingots left buried on the island:

> The bar silver and the arms still lie, for all that I know, where Flint buried them; and certainly they shall lie there for me. Oxen and wain-ropes would not bring me back again to that accursed island.

8. *The Merchant of Venice*: the pound of flesh, the Kingdom of Belmont, and the hermeneutics of Socrates

Shakespeare, too, imagined a realm immune from the fever of profit. He chose the hinterland of the Veneto as the setting for one of the two scenarios for *The Merchant of Venice*. In the imaginary realm of Belmont, gold and silver are held in contempt, as is evinced by the verses contained in the casket connected with the future husband of the wise and beautiful Portia. The prince of Morocco—who opts to open the golden casket bearing the legend "Who chooseth me shall gain what many men desire"—instead of finding the portrait of the longed-for spouse, is mocked by the verses penned on a parchment inserted in the "empty eye" of "carrion Death":

> All that glitters is not gold;
> Often have you heard that told:
> Many a man his life hath sold
> But my outside to behold:
> Gilded tombs do worms enfold.
> Had you been as wise as bold,
> Young in limbs, in judgment old,
> Your answer had not been inscroll'd:
> Fare you well; your suit is cold.

The same fate awaits the prince of Arragon, attracted by the silver casket on which is engraved the promise "Who chooseth me shall get as much as he deserves." And, instead of Portia, he receives in exchange a stinging rebuke:

> The fire seven times tried this:
> Seven times tried that judgment is,
> That did never choose amiss.
> Some there be that shadows kiss;
> Such have but a shadow's bliss:
> There be fools alive, I wis,
> Silver'd o'er; and so was this.
> Take what wife you will to bed,
> I will ever be your head:
> So be gone: you are sped.

Among the suitors, only the "humanist" Bassanio makes the right choice. His words, in fact, seem to anticipate the verses he finds hidden shortly afterward in the lead casket, on which is engraved the warning "Who chooseth me must give and hazard all he hath":

> So may the outward shows be least themselves:
> The world is still deceived with ornament.
> In law, what plea so tainted and corrupt,
> But, being seasoned with a gracious voice,
> Obscures the show of evil? In religion,
> What damned error, but some sober brow
> Will bless it and approve it with a text,
> Hiding the grossness with fair ornament?
> There is no vice so simple but assumes
> Some mark of virtue on his outward parts:
> How many cowards, whose hearts are all as false
> As stairs of sand, wear yet upon their chins
> The beards of Hercules and frowning Mars;
> Who, inward search'd, have livers white as milk;
> And these assume but valour's excrement . . .

Bassanio does not like amassing money and does not look after his assets ("'Tis not unknown to you, Antonio, / How much I have disabled mine estate, / By something showing a more swelling port / Than my faint means would grant continuance"). And although, at first, marriage with Portia might seem a stratagem for the repayment of his debts (as he confesses, "To you, Antonio, / I owe the most, in money and in love, / And from your love I have a warranty / To unburden all my plots and purposes / How to get clear of all the debts

I owe"), when he stands in front of the caskets in the imaginary residence, the suitor expresses a view of the world centered on the dialectic of reality-appearances. For the young Venetian, the exterior aspect of what appears before our eyes is deceptive. You must be able to see beyond the surface to understand that lies are often disguised as truth and that countless perils lurk beneath the splendor of gold and silver:

> Thus ornament is but the guiled shore
> To a most dangerous sea; the beauteous scarf
> Veiling an Indian beauty; in a word,
> The seeming truth which cunning times put on
> To entrap the wisest. Therefore, thou gaudy gold,
> Hard food for Midas, I will none of thee;
> Nor none of thee, thou pale and common drudge
> 'Tween man and man: but thou, thou meagre lead,
> Which rather threatenest than dost promise aught,
> Thy paleness moves me more than eloquence;
> And here choose I; joy be the consequence!

It is no accident that in the humblest casket, the lead one, Bassanio finds the portrait of his beloved and the verses that reward his wisdom: "You that choose not by the view,/Chance as fair and choose as true!" The lover, in short, wins Portia by looking to the example of Socrates, who had inspired various Renaissance authors (including Pico della Mirandola, Erasmus, Rabelais, Ronsard, Tasso, and Giordano Bruno). Based on the *topos* of Socrates the Silene as described by Alcibiades in the *Symposium*, this image became a hermeneutic instrument for explaining the way texts and the world work: you must necessarily get past the exterior to find, behind appearances, the true essence of things. To cut a long story short, appearances do not count. A precept that holds not only for judging words, but also things and people.

In Venice, instead, the dominant values are the opposite of those of Belmont. There—within a context in which a series of social and religious conflicts arise—the themes of usury and commerce dominate the scene to such an extent that even human beings are equated with goods and cash. In order to help Bassanio, Antonio borrows three thousand ducats from the Jew Shylock. The Venetian merchant is well aware of the risk he is taking (his creditor is portrayed as a Silene in reverse: "An evil soul producing holy witness/Is like a villain with a smiling cheek,/A goodly apple rotten at the heart:/O, what a goodly outside falsehood hath!"). The penalty agreed upon is not in cash, but consists of a pound of flesh that the creditor himself can collect by cutting into the debtor's body ("Let the forfeit/Be nominated for an equal pound/Of your fair flesh, to be cut off and taken/In what part of your body pleaseth me"). And being unable to honor the contract, on account of the failure of his ships to arrive, Antonio is dragged into court by the rich usurer who, expecting no less ("I will have the heart of him"), demands that the terms of the contract be respected.

The inhumanity that Shylock is accused of more than once finds its echo in the inhumanity that, in the previous scene, the Jew had accused the Christians of:

> Hath not a Jew eyes? hath not a Jew hands, organs,
> dimensions, senses, affections, passions? fed with
> the same food, hurt with the same weapons, subject
> to the same diseases, healed by the same means,
> warmed and cooled by the same winter and summer, as
> a Christian is? If you prick us, do we not bleed?
> if you tickle us, do we not laugh? if you poison
> us, do we not die? and if you wrong us, shall we not
> revenge?

It is up to Portia—in the guise of Balthazar, "doctor of laws"—to find a solution to the dispute. The contract must be respected to the letter. Shylock must cut out his due with precision: one pound of flesh, without a drop of blood, but not one gram too much, nor one gram too little. The forfeit will be measured on a goldsmith's scales, and a minimal variation will cost Shylock his life and his goods:

> Therefore prepare thee to cut off the flesh.
> Shed thou no blood, nor cut thou less nor more
> But just a pound of flesh: if thou cut'st more
> Or less than a just pound, be it but so much
> As makes it light or heavy in the substance,
> Or the division of the twentieth part
> Of one poor scruple, nay, if the scale do turn
> But in the estimation of a hair,
> Thou diest and all thy goods are confiscate.

The blood of a citizen of Venice must not be shed,

of course. But, at the same time, it is precisely the *surplus* (what is in excess) or any variation in *measure* (what is lacking) that dissuades the creditor from demanding that the contract be respected to the letter.

At least for a moment, Portia reminds Shylock and Antonio that the laws of the market and usury cannot transform men into goods. Be they Jews or Christians—the fake Balthazar deliberately does not distinguish one from the other: "Which is the merchant here, and which the Jew?"—no contract authorizes anyone to equate human flesh with any kind of product on the market. Life, contrary to what the creditor thinks, does not coincide with money ("[Y]ou take my life / when you do take the means whereby I live"). And the beautiful lady from the Kingdom of Belmont bears witness to this in person when she refuses any payment for her work ("He is well paid that is well satisfied; / And I, delivering you, am satisfied / And therein do account myself well paid: / My mind was never yet more mercenary").

Indirect proof of the centrality of the theme of usury and money in this play also comes from the shrewd analysis made by Karl Marx, who evokes Shylock in various works. Leaving aside the controversial interpretation of his concept of the "Jewish question," Marx was convinced that the protagonist of *The Merchant of Venice* becomes the embodiment of capitalism, marking the shift "from the usurer to the modern creditor." So the ghost of Shylock—which has nothing to do with the Jew in flesh and blood—becomes, in his writings on usury, a metaphor for capital and the alienation of man

reduced to cash and goods. In his essay "Marx and Shylock," Luciano Parinetto explains that:

> Like the Jew, like Shylock, the nationality of capital
> is chimerical because it respects no one, and this has
> no frontiers: inside or outside the nation it claims its
> *pound of flesh*. This is why the fictional Jew, stateless
> by definition, personifies it in such an exemplary fash-
> ion. It is further confirmation of what Marx had writ-
> ten in 1843: "The chimerical nationality of the Jew is
> the nationality of the merchant, of the man of money
> in general."

In light of the ambiguous play of opposites that
Shakespeare skillfully stages in this mysterious and
complex comedy, I believe that the hermeneutics of
Socrates may help to grasp the inversion of reality
and appearances, truth and fiction. This is a game, as
Franco Marenco has rightly emphasized, which also in-
volves the very essence of the word, whose meaning os-
cillates between the literal and figurative sense. Thus
the themes of usury, trade, debit and credit, squander-
ing and accumulating, mercy, heterosexual and homo-
sexual love, melancholy and joy, conflict between Jews
and Christians, religious tensions between radicals and
moderates, and ambiguous relations between the op-
pressed and their oppressors, all refer back to the dialectic relation between *res* and *verba* (*intus* and *extra*)
that dominates all aspects of the play.

The same scene can have a different meaning. Everything depends on the point of view from which the ac-
tions and words of the players are interpreted. The Jew

Shylock is victim and tormentor at the same time, while the same holds for the Christians who clash with him. Faced with the same situation, there are some who laugh and some who weep (Portia's allusion to the "weeping philosopher" certainly refers to the *topos* of Heraclitus and Democritus). The comic and the tragic coexist in the same space: for the characters (on the stage) and the spectators (in the theater of the world), that single scene can arouse joy in some and sorrow in others. Uncertainty and relativity, as Agostino Lombardo has pointed out, inform the entire shape of the work.

Many other important questions ought to be brought up and discussed. But in this brief reflection all I wanted to do was analyze one of the many threads that might link Venice and the imaginary realm of Belmont, in which gold and silver are worth nothing compared to birdsong or the beauty of nature. Lorenzo, in harmony with some of Portia's thoughts, expresses this clearly when he maintains that a man insensitive to music can easily fall victim to the utilitarian violence of deceit and rapine:

> The man that hath no music in himself,
> Nor is not moved with concord of sweet sounds,
> Is fit for treasons, stratagems and spoils;
> The motions of his spirit are dull as night
> And his affections dark as Erebus:
> Let no such man be trusted. Mark the music.

Here—in this imaginary *island* invented by Shakespeare where, as the lead casket reminds us, *giving* is worth more than *having*—the gratuitous and the useless seem shielded from the destructive power of the god money, and from the most inhuman utilitarianism that condemns men to become the slaves of profit and to transform themselves into ordinary goods . . .

9. Aristotle: learning has no practical usefulness

Culture, too, should be protected from the corrosive power of money and profit. With regard to the intrinsic worth of learning, Aristotle had some important things to say in his *Metaphysics*. He was the one to formulate clearly the idea that learning at the highest levels is not "a productive science." And moreover "both in our day and since the beginning, it is thanks to their sense of wonder that men began to philosophize." It was precisely their amazement on account of those "phenomena that were within reach and could not be explained" that prompted them to embark on the quest. And so "while it is true that men began to philosophize with a view to eluding ignorance, it is clear that they were pursuing knowledge solely for its own sake, and not for any practical need":

> Clearly, therefore, we devote ourselves to such inquiry without aiming at any need extraneous to it, but, just as we call him who exists for his own sake and not for another's a free man, so we consider such knowledge as the only kind that is free, since it alone exists for its own sake.

This freedom of philosophy, characterized by the refusal to be a slave to the useful, is the foundation of the *divinitas* of human beings ("And so we can justly hold the possession of it as beyond human power").

10. Pure theorist or philosopher-king? Plato's contradictions

Aristotle, in short, neatly resolves the constant dialectic tension that exists in Plato between the philosopher interested in pure speculation and the philosopher involved in politics. In the *Theaetetus*, in fact, Socrates makes a distinction between "slaves" or "servants" and "free men," between those who frequent the courts and those interested exclusively in philosophy:

> In comparison with those whose background is in philosophy and similar studies, those who have frequented the courts and the like since their youth risk looking more like slaves than free men.

"Free men" have no problems with time and have to account to no one, whereas "servants" are ruled by the clock and by a *master* who decides:

> Free men, no doubt, as you said, always have time at their disposal, and hold their discourse at their leisure ... To them it matters nothing if their words are many or few, provided they can grasp the essence. Others, instead, never have much time available, because the clock drives them on and they are not able to discuss the argument as they would wish. And their adversary presses them with the inexorability of the laws and the indictment to be read out: over and above these limits it is not permitted to speak. And their

discourse, which always regards a fellow-slave, is addressed to a master who, seated, holds some punishment in his hands.

These last, spurred on by the goal to be attained, "learn to fawn on the master, flattering him, and winning his benevolence with facts." Thus, being "petty of soul," they give up all forms of rectitude:

> Having been slaves since youth deprives them of any chance of moral growth, upright conduct and nobility of sentiment, obliging them to act in a twisted manner, thus making spirits that are still delicate face great risks and great fears, which they cannot sustain together with justice and truth, but, by turning instantly to the lie and mutual insult, they bend and break into many pieces, and so their mind is in no wise sound when they pass from youth into manhood, having become—or so they think—expert and wise.

"True philosophers," instead, "from youth onward, have never known the way to the square, or the tribunal, or the council building, or any other public meeting place in the city." They know nothing about intrigues aimed at securing public positions, or attending "meetings, lunches, or parties where young ladies play the flute." They deem "all these things to be of scant value, or indeed of no value at all" and spread their wings "studying the stars, *up there in the sky*, and exploring from all sides the entire nature of existing things." And when "such a man talks to someone in private or in public" it can easily happen that he "causes the laughter not only of Thracian handmaidens, but also of people in general" and thus his awkwardness earns him a name for stupidity. To walk the path of true philosophy, as Paul Ricoeur has pointed out, also means exposing yourself to failure as far as life is concerned. But, in his bid to win freedom, the true philosopher always tries to keep his gaze trained on the heavens and does not fear the risk of ending up, like Thales, in a well:

> Well, Theodorus, these are the characters of both: one is that of the man truly raised in freedom and the availability of time, the man that you call a philosopher, who does not think it blameworthy to appear ingenuous and to be considered a nobody when he may have to perform menial tasks, for example, because he does not know how to prepare a traveling bag with bed linen, or how to season food, or how to make flattering speeches. The other, for his part, is he who is capable of performing all these tasks speedily and easily, but does not know how to flip his cloak over his right shoulder like a free man, or to sing hymns suitable to the true life of the gods and happy men.

In the *Republic*, however, Plato had already analyzed the two attitudes, giving us a glimpse of the possibility that a philosopher may have a commitment to public life. Socrates reminds his interlocutor of the importance of pure research, an end in itself: "not even they [the majority] have listened to enough fine and noble discussions in which every effort is made to seek the truth, for the sole purpose of learning." And further on, in a context dominated by the theme of the education of youngsters, he returns to the argument, stressing the necessity that teaching must not take the form of "an obligation to learn," because "a free man must learn nothing in a servile spirit."

But, as Mario Vegetti has made very clear, there are various cases of philosopher-rulers in the *Republic*. And it is precisely those philosophers who educate themselves, through private study, and who are prompted by the exclusive desire to know—in the *Theaetetus* there is mention also of the Hesiodic myth of Iris (philosophy), the daughter of Thaumas (wonder)—who Plato asks *exceptionally* to reign (*basileuein*): it is up to them to form the *archontes* and the dialecticians who will govern the future city.

11. Kant: the pleasure of beauty is disinterested

Starting with Immanuel Kant, the question of selflessness was to involve esthetic judgment, too. In the opening pages of the *Critique of Judgment* (1790), the German philosopher maintained that the appreciation of a representation of an object can be accompanied by pleasure "no matter how indifferent I may be to the real existence of the object of this representation":

> It is quite plain that in order to say that the object is beautiful, and to show that I have taste, everything turns on the meaning which I can give to this representation, and not on any factor which makes me dependent on the real existence of the object . . . This proposition, which is of the utmost importance, cannot be better explained than by contrasting the pure disin-

terested delight which appears in the judgment of taste
with that allied to an interest.

For Kant, interest is closely connected with pleasure
and the existence of the object. And given that "all interest presupposes a want, or calls one forth; and, being
a ground determining approval, deprives the judgment
on the object of its freedom," only "taste in the beautiful may be said to be the one and only disinterested and
free delight; for, with it, no interest, whether of sense or
reason, extorts approval." So, basing himself precisely
on this notion of disinterest, Kant went on to formulate
his renowned definition of taste:

> *Taste* is the faculty of estimating an object or a mode of
> representation by means of a delight or aversion *apart
> from any interest*. The object of such a delight is called
> *beautiful*.

12. Ovid: nothing is more useful
than the useless arts

Among the literati, Ovid (a vigilant and severe critic
in *Metamorphoses* of the "infamous passion for possession") explicitly tackles the question of the usefulness of
the useless. In one of the *Epistulae ex Ponto*—addressed
to his friend Aurelius Cotta Maximus Messalinus—
the poet confesses that he cultivates the useless: "The
answer to your question is that nothing is more useful/
than this art that has no usefulness" ("Cum bene quae-
sieris quid agam, magis utile nil est/artibus his, quae
nil utilitatis habent").

Although Ovid occasionally considered poetry as a remedy for the pangs of exile ("From it I may forget my misfortune"), he was well aware that you can gain no true advantage from poetry: "To this day none of all the works I have made has been of use to me—if only none of them had proved harmful!" Indeed, it is precisely to his verses, perhaps, that we should ascribe the causes of his misfortunes.

Despite everything, however, faced with the question regarding the reasons for his writing—"So why do I write, you will say"—the poet does not hesitate to reply "I continue to ply a useless trade," as happens to the gladiator who, despite his wounds, takes up arms once more or the sailor who, although he has been shipwrecked, returns to sea.

13. Montaigne: "nothing is useless," "not even uselessness itself"

No book can shake our innermost being like Montaigne's *Essays* (1580–88). Yet the author declares that he did not write them for any precise end ("I did not intend [this book] to have any purpose, other than domestic and private") but to give an intimate account, as has been brilliantly suggested by Fausta Garavini, of the fears and the defenses "of a being who discovers that he is fragmented and diversified": "So, reader, I myself am the matter of my book: there is no reason why you should waste your time on such a frivolous and vain subject." A *useless* book, therefore, which is conceived in the library, constructed right where a ward-

robe once stood, "the most useless place in the house."
It is here that Montaigne passed most of his time, in
solitude, studying for fun and not for profit ("[I stud-
ied] Now, for my amusement. Never for profit"). And
he studied knowing perfectly well that philosophy is
considered to be something "of no use and no value":

> It is very strange that in our day things have come to
> the point that philosophy is, even for persons of intel-
> lect, a vain and fantastic name, a thing of no use and
> no value.

But, despite this, Montaigne does not lay down his
arms. Indeed, on diverse occasions, he invites us to recognize the uselessness of those goods commonly held
to be useful (we ought to "stimulate in men a contempt
for gold and silk as vain and useless things; instead we
increase the honor and value [in which they are held],
which is a truly foolish way to disgust men").

The author of the *Essays* knew well that many of his
"best qualities" were completely useless "in a very depraved age":

> In this age I would have found even the best qualities I
> possess to be useless. The liberality of my habits would
> have been called slackness or weakness; my faith and
> conscience would have been thought scrupulous and
> superstitious; my frankness and independence, impor-
> tune, ill-considered, and rash.

Far from any pretensions, the *Essays* are presented as
a statement. And the concern of his family—who were
afraid that young Michel's future would be character-

ized by uselessness ("No one predicted that I should become wicked, merely useless")—was not so far off the
mark, given the precocious signs of a strong interest in
the business of writing:

> There should be, however, some legal constraint against
> inept and useless writers, as there is against vagabonds
> and good-for-nothings. Both I and a hundred others
> would be banished, left beyond the reach of our people.
> I am not joking.

Of course, we should not always take Montaigne literally, as André Tournon wisely suggests in comment-
ing on the abovementioned passages. But the awareness
of his *uselessness* ("Finding myself of no use to this age,
I turn to another one"), can coexist perfectly well with
his conviction that "there is nothing useless in nature,"
"not even uselessness itself."

14. Leopardi the flâneur: the choice of the useless against the utilitarianism of a "proud and foolish age"

Between 1831 and 1832 Giacomo Leopardi, together
with his dear friend Antonio Ranieri, planned a weekly
paper (*Lo Spettatore Fiorentino*), which he wanted to be
useless. In the Preamble in fact, the author declares: "Let
us confess frankly that our Paper will have no utility." In
an age entirely devoted to the useful, it was of fundamental importance to draw the attention to the useless:

> And we think it reasonable that in an age in which all
> books, all pieces of printed paper, all visiting cards are

useful, that finally there should be a Paper that pro-
fesses to be useless: because man tends to distinguish
himself from the others, and because, when all is useful, one may promise the useless for the purpose of
speculation.

Convinced that the "pleasurable is more useful than
the useful," Leopardi thought that women, indifferent to any logic of production, represented the weekly's
ideal readership. And he did not do so out of gallantry,
but because "women, being less severe, may likely treat
our uselessness more kindly." The project, naturally, did
not obtain the necessary permission from the Floren-
tine authorities and was stillborn.

A few years before, in 1827, Leopardi had been
working on an *Enciclopedia delle cognizioni inutili* (En-
cyclopedia of Useless Knowledge), another idea that
never got off the drawing board, which he talks about
in a letter to the publisher Stella dated 13 July 1827.
His lively interest in uselessness is the expression of the
uneasiness of a man of letters who finds himself living
in a society dominated by "storekeepers and other men
devoted to making money." A society in which people
come to coincide with money:

> Almost as if men, disagreeing in all other opinions,
> agree only in the esteem of money: or almost as if
> money were in substance the man; and nothing else
> but money: something that a thousand pointers seem
> to indicate that humankind holds as a constant axiom,
> especially in our day . . . In the meantime, along with
> industry, baseness of the spirit, coldness, egoism, ava-

rice, falsity, and mercantile perfidy, all of uncivilized man's most depraved and unworthy qualities and passions are in force and multiply endlessly; but virtues are a long time coming.

Through his philosophy of the useless, Leopardi did not wish only to defend the survival of thought (it is necessary to promise "the useless for the purpose of speculation"), but he also wishes to vindicate the importance of life, literature, love, the deceits of poetry, and all those things held to be superfluous. In a letter sent from Florence to Pietro Giordani on 24 July 1828, Leopardi wrote:

> In short it is beginning to turn my stomach [when I think of] the haughty contempt that is professed here for all things beautiful and all literature: in particular, I cannot get it through my head that the height of human learning lies in knowing about politics and statistics. Indeed, considering philosophically the almost perfect uselessness of studies made since the age of Solon onward to obtain the perfection of civil states and the happiness of peoples, I feel a little like laughing at this vogue for calculations and political and legislative ploys . . . So it happens that the pleasurable seems to me to be more useful than all other utility, and literature more truly and certainly useful than all these dry-as-dust disciplines [politics and statistics].

But Leopardi, as he himself was to point out in some verses in "The Ruling Thought," knew he was living in a period that was "an enemy to virtue," in which the obsessive search for utility had ended up making life itself useless ("As for this proud age, / which feeds on empty hopes,/and idle prattle, an enemy to virtue;/this foolish age, crying out for utility,/that cannot see how useless it will make life;/I feel greater than that . . ." Such utilitarianism, linked to a mistaken idea of progress, was hailed ever more frequently by the press, as Leopardi himself was to declare in the "Palinode to Marquis Gino Capponi" ("All the papers,/in all languages and types,/agree to promise the entire world/ Universal love,/railroads and commerce of all kinds;/ steam, printing presses, and cholera/will unite the peoples of all climes." And for these reasons, shortly before his death, in a decisive verse from "The Ginestra" he was to describe his age as "proud and foolish."

15. Théophile Gautier: "what is useful is ugly" as "the jakes"

A few years after Leopardi's singular plan for a useless weekly, Théophile Gautier was to take to its extreme consequences the battle against the dominant prudery of some "utilitarian critics" ("authentic literary cops" ready "to grab and beat up, in the name of virtue, every idea that circulates in a book with its cap slightly askew or its skirt drawn up a little too high"), egged on and sponsored by the newspapers ("of whatever color they may be, red, green, or tricolor") who offered themselves as "useful."

In 1834, aged twenty-three, Gautier wrote a long preface to his novel *Mademoiselle de Maupin*, which not only became the manifesto of the so-called "Art for Art's Sake" movement, but more generally the eloquent reaction of a generation in revolt against those "who claim to be economists and wish to reconstruct society from top to bottom":

> No, imbeciles, no, cretins and goitered fools that you are, you can't make trifle with a book; a novel is not a pair of seamless boots; a sonnet is not a continuous jet of water; a play is not a railroad: all superbly civilizing things that cause humanity to march along the road to progress.

Accused by the daily *Le Constitutionnel* of writing indecent articles, Gautier replied brilliantly to the insults with a language that was ironic, scornful, full of metaphors and allusions. It is a dazzling pamphlet in which the author, over and above the occasional polemic, expresses his poetics, based essentially on an idea of art and literature free of all moral and utilitarian conditioning:

> On listening to the dissertations of republican utilitarians and the worthy followers of Saint-Simon you really feel like laughing your head off . . . There are two kinds of utility, and the meaning of that word is always relative. What is useful for one person is not so for another. You are a cobbler, I am a poet. For me it is useful for my first line to rhyme with the second. A rhyming dictionary is very useful to me, while you cannot use one to sole an old pair of boots, and I must say that a shoemaker's knife would not be of much use to me in composing an ode. After this, you will object that a cobbler is superior to a poet and that we can do without the latter more easily than the former. Without trying to disparage the cobbler's illustrious trade, which I honor

as much as that of constitutional monarch, I humbly confess that I would rather have a shoe whose upper has come away than a poorly rhymed verse, and that I would willingly do without boots rather than poetry.

Gautier, whose poetic skills Jean Starobinski has metaphorically compared to those of an acrobat, insists frequently on the fact that, unfortunately, in the pages of those newspapers, the beautiful things in life are not considered indispensable, to the point that it is held to be more useful to plant cabbages instead of tulips:

> Nothing beautiful is indispensable to life. If someone put an end to flowers, the world would not suffer in a material fashion; but who would wish for there to be no more flowers? I would give up potatoes far more willingly than roses, and I believe that only a utilitarian would be capable of destroying a bed of tulips in order to plant cabbages.

In this context dominated by the crassest utilitarianism, it is no surprise if you run the risk of being considered a lunatic if you dare to prefer Michelangelo over the "inventor of white mustard" ("What is the use of music? What is the use of painting? Who would be mad enough to prefer Mozart to Carrel [a journalist with *Le National*] and Michelangelo to the inventor of white mustard")? As it is no surprise if in utilitarian papers books are advertised together with "elastic belts, crinoline collars, babies' bottles with undeformable teats, M. Regnault's paste, and toothache remedies."

But Gautier was convinced that it was not enough to combat this rampant triviality with an understated reaction. On the contrary, exploiting his paradoxical style, he drives home his attack on utilitarianism by singing the praises of the useless in a provocative and radical manner:

> The only truly beautiful things are useless; everything useful is ugly, because it is the expression of a certain need, and man's needs are ignoble and disgusting, as is his wretched, infirm nature. The most useful place in the home is the toilet.

It would be really interesting—and I believe that this has never been done with any care—to analyze these pages of Gautier's on the useless in parallel with those of Leopardi. And, among the many convergences, we should certainly not overlook the presence of Vesuvius. In point of fact, in his preface, Gautier also brings up the volcano and the Roman cities buried by the eruption (Leopardi's "Ginestra" was written in 1836 but published posthumously in 1845), as testimony to contemporary pseudo-progress:

> Ah, you say we are progressing! If tomorrow the mouth of a volcano were to open wide in Montmartre, and spread over Paris a shroud of ashes and a sepulcher of lava, as Vesuvius did in times gone by in Stabia, Pompeii, and Herculaneum, and if, within a few thousand years' time, archaeologists were to excavate and unearth the dead city, what monument, tell me, would still be standing to bear witness to the great buried one?

Centuries afterward, archaeologists would have unearthed only industrial products or mass produced items. And, apart from a few exceptions, the true works of art would be the exclusive expression of earlier millennia. This is why, for Gautier, superficial objects, those things that have no utility insofar as they are expressions of beauty, will turn out to be the most interesting and pleasing of all:

> Whether or not these gentlemen approve, I am one of those people for whom the superfluous is necessary, and I love things and people in inverse proportion to what services they may render me. Compared to a certain vase that is useful I prefer a Chinese one, covered with dragons and mandarins, which is of no use to me at all . . . I would gladly give up my rights as a Frenchman and a citizen to see a genuine Raphael . . . Even though I am a music lover, I prefer the sound of out of tune violins and tambourines with jingles to that of the chairman's bell. I would sell my pants to have a ring, and bread to have sweets . . . It's very easy to see that utilitarian principles are far from my own, and that I will never be an editor with a virtuous newspaper.

Two years previously, in the preface to *Albertus*, Gautier had expressed similar concepts. And to those who asked him the use of a rhyme, he had replied by opposing beauty to utility:

> What use is this? Its use is to be beautiful. Not enough? Like flowers, like perfumes, like birds, like all the things that man has been unable to redirect and pervert to his service. In general, as soon as something becomes useful it ceases to be beautiful.

In the two prefaces, as a skillful manipulator of the language, the young writer offers a poetic expression of his critical thinking. In the preface to *Mademoiselle de Maupin*, in particular—where the novelist vies with the poet—he colors verbs and adjectives, fashions metaphors and neologisms, and talks about art, making use above all of prose that is felicitous and creative. But it would be a mistake to reduce his manifesto solely to a eulogy on beauty as an end in itself. In his furious reaction to the fanaticism of "utility for utility's sake," to prudery and literature that prostitutes itself to trade, there still emerges a noble idea of true art as a form of resistance to the triviality of the present. "Art," Gautier confesses in the closing sentence of the preface to *Albertus*, "is the best consolation for living."

16. Baudelaire: a useful man is a squalid one

In the fragments of *My Heart Laid Bare*, Baudelaire (who dedicated *Les fleurs du mal* to Théophile Gautier, "the perfect magician of French literature") makes a remark thanks to which his rejection of utilitarianism emerges even more strongly: "To be a useful man has always struck me as squalid." Similar reflections are also to be found in the drafts of *Fusées* (Rockets) that should have constituted, together with *My Heart Laid Bare*, the basis of a work open to a pitiless journey through the uneasiness of living.

A clear sign of the contemporary "debasement of hearts," for Baudelaire, was to see young people rushing toward commerce with the sole aim of making money:

So the son will flee the family, no longer at eighteen but at twelve years, emancipated by his gluttonous precocity. He will flee it not to seek heroic adventures, not to free a beautiful maiden from a tower, not to immortalize a slum with sublime thoughts, but to establish a business, to get rich, to compete against his infamous father . . .

And while everything will be subject to criticism and condemnation "except money," all things that "resemble virtue" will be considered "hugely laughable." Even justice "will disqualify those citizens who have not made a fortune." Corruption will pervade families to such a point that wives and daughters will become a base means of exchange:

> Your wife, O bourgeois! Your chaste partner, whose legitimacy is the only note of poetry in your life, by legalizing impeccable infamy, this vigilant and loving guardian of your strongbox will no longer be other than the perfect ideal of the kept woman. Your daughter, with her infantile dream of marriage, will dream from the cradle of being sold for a million. And you, O bourgeois, even less of a poet than you are today, will find nothing wrong with that; you will have no regrets.

In the closing remarks to *My Heart Laid Bare*, Baudelaire expresses all his disdain for trade and the most trivial forms of egoism:

> Commerce is essentially *satanic*.
>> —Commerce is the loan returned, in other words the loan that carries the unspoken rider: *give me back more than I gave*.
>> —The soul of every merchant is completely rotten.

—Commerce is natural, hence infamous.

—The least infamous of all traders is the one who says: "Let us be virtuous so we can make much more money than the fools who are not."

—For the trader, honesty itself is a form of speculation aimed at making a profit.

—Commerce is satanic because it is one of the forms of egoism: the basest and the vilest.

This world, that of utilitarianism and profit, is not the kind of place where poetry and intimacy may find a place: "thanks to the progress of our times, all that will remain of your insides will be the viscera!"

17. John Locke against poetry

Conversely, John Locke based his attack on poetry precisely on uselessness. In *Some Thoughts Concerning Education* (1693), his criticism is not directed solely at those who at all costs oblige idle students to study poetry in order to make modest versifiers of them ("for, if he has no genius to poetry, it is the most unreasonable thing in the world to torment a child, and waste his time about that which can never succeed"), but concerns above all those parents who allow their children to cultivate their poetic talent ("and if he have a poetic vein, it is to me the strangest thing in the world, that the father should desire or suffer it to be cherished or improved"). Because life amid the Muses, on Mount Parnassus, is a hard one and in no way favors the growth of one's personal estate:

Methinks the parents should labour to have it stifled
and suppressed as much as may be; and I know not
what reason a father can have to wish his son a poet,
who does not desire to have him bid defiance to all
other callings and business; which is not yet the worst
of the case; for if he proves a successful rhymer, and
gets once the reputation of a wit, I desire it may be considered, what company and places he is like to spend his
time in, nay, and estate too; for it is very seldom seen,
that any one discovers mines of gold or silver in Parnassus. It is a pleasant air, but a barren soil; and there
are very few instances of those who have added to their
patrimony by any thing they have reaped from thence.

As a matter of fact, Locke's principal goal was to
make a gentleman, favoring technical and scientific
knowledge based on pragmatism and utility. His fero-
cious reaction, however, cannot be understood without
taking into account the fanaticism of a rhetorical pedagogy whereby the England of his day found words more
important than things. But, today, what effect might
his railing against poetry (I shall spare the reader his
invective against music) have on the many politicians
and manager-pedagogues involved in the most recent
educational reforms? It is hard to answer this question
with any certainty. My experience as a teacher in an
arts faculty—where for decades we have heard the same
question from parents who are a prey to the pernicious
and dominant ideology of utility: "Yes, but what's my
son/daughter going to do with a degree in literature?"—
leads me to suppose that, probably, Locke's caustic arguments would ruffle no one's feathers.

18. Boccaccio: "bread" and poetry

Keeping company with the Muses—who Giovanni Boccaccio identifies with women in flesh and blood—helps us to live better. In the *Decameron*, Boccaccio argues with his detractors, obsessed with the search for "treasures," who invite him to think about "bread" rather than the "poets' fables":

> But what to say to those who pity me so much for my hunger that they advise me to get my hands on some bread? I don't know, but when I try to imagine what their answer might be if I, out of need, should ask them for some, I think they would tell me to go look for it in my fables. Indeed, in times gone by poets have found more bread in their fables than many a rich man in his treasures, and so many, by pursuing their fables, have brought luster on their age; whereas, on the contrary, in seeking to have more bread than they needed, many have come to a bitter end.

"The poets' fables," independently of the amount of "bread" they make it possible to acquire, are required to understand the essential things we need. And, above all, they teach us to defend ourselves from the obsession for gain and profit that, as happens to those who hunt for riches, often becomes the cause of a premature death.

19. García Lorca: it is unwise to live without the madness of poetry

Over the centuries, many poets and men of letters have indirectly replied to Locke and the detractors of poetry.

But, in particular, the words of Federico García Lorca, in introducing some poems by Pablo Neruda, strike a chord in our hearts:

> I advise you to listen carefully to this great poet and to try to be moved along with him; each in his own way. Poetry requires a lengthy initiation, like any sport, but in real poetry there is a perfume, an accent, a luminous trait that all creatures can perceive. And, God willing, may this serve to nourish that grain of madness we all have inside, and that many kill in order to don the hateful monocle of bookish pedantry and without which it is unwise to live.

This impassioned testimony, in which one great poet talks about another great poet, was intended above all for the students present in a lecture hall of Madrid University in 1934. To those young readers, García Lorca addressed a warm invitation to nourish with literature "that grain of madness we all have inside" and without which it would really be "unwise to live."

20. The madness of Don Quixote, the hero of the useless and the gratuitous

And it is precisely to madness that we owe the extraordinary adventures of one of the characters who has left his mark on the history of world literature. The legendary Don Quixote could be considered the hero of uselessness par excellence. Raised on chivalric romances, he decides to twist the corrupt reality of his day in which "vice [triumphs over] virtue":

Nonetheless, our depraved age does not deserve the blessings enjoyed in the days when knights errant defended realms, protected damsels, gave support to orphans and minors, punished the proud, and rewarded the humble!

Contrary to the opinion of his contemporaries—so convinced that "all the books on chivalry are false, mendacious, harmful, and *useless* to the republic" that they were prepared to cast them into the flames remorselessly—the courageous hidalgo did not hesitate to take the hard road of the cavalier, persuaded that "the thing the world needs most is knights errant and that in him [Don Quixote himself] knight errantry had been brought back to life." Careless of physical limitations ("lean in build with sharp features"), and the limitations of his weapons and his tinny armor ("The first thing he did was to clean up the arms that had belonged to his grandfather, which, eaten by rust and mildew, had lain forgotten for long centuries in some corner"), or the limitations of his nag (whose "hooves had more cracks than an ancient coin and more ailments than Gonella's horse," which was so much skin and bone), our hero set forth upon "paths that were not paths at all."

All his deeds were inspired by selflessness, by the sole need to serve his ideals with enthusiasm. And in the conversations with Sancho Panza and those others he meets from time to time—in which, very often, there emerge the reservations of a society that cannot conceive of acts unconnected with some utilitarian end—Don Quixote confesses that he holds riches in contempt ("I despise wealth") and that only honor is important to him. Moreover, how could we imagine love without selflessness? Knights errant must protect their beloved "without their thoughts ever straying beyond the pure service owed to her for her own sake, without hoping in any other prize for their good and numerous desires except that she willingly accept them as her knights."

Cervantes, in short, makes contradiction one of the great themes of his novel: if the invective against books of chivalry sounds like an incitement to disillusion, in *Don Quixote* we also find a eulogy to illusion that, through the passion for ideals, manages to give a meaning to life. It is no accident, as the great Cervantes expert Francisco Rico has pointed out, that our hero expresses an extraordinary love of narrative and shows an avid interest in the lives of others. In any case, the uselessness and selflessness of Don Quixote's adventures leave their mark: they reveal the need to face with courage even those enterprises doomed to failure. There are glorious defeats from which, in time, great things may be born ("The truth stretches and grows thin, but it does not break and always floats on top of falsehood, like oil on water").

Who would ever have thought that the defiant gesture of the Chinese youth facing off a tank in Tiananmen Square in 1989—immortalized by the photographer Jeff Widener—would have gone right around the world to be hailed by *Time* magazine, almost ten years later in 1998, as one of the exploits that have most influenced the twentieth century?

21. The Facts of Coketown: Dickens's criticism of utilitarianism

Charles Dickens has given us the finest portrayal of the war declared on imagination in the name of facts and utilitarianism. In the memorable city of Coketown, wonderfully described in *Hard Times*, all things are subordinated to the philosophy of utility. The fat banker Bounderby and the teacher Gradgrind fight a dogged daily battle against anything that might hinder practicality and production.

"In this life, we want nothing but Facts, sir; nothing but Facts!" The enemy of teaching open to imagination, sentiments, and affection, Gradgrind is introduced "with a rule and a pair of scales, and the multiplication table always in his pocket . . . ready to weigh and measure any parcel of human nature, and tell you exactly what it comes to." For him, education and life are reduced to a "mere question of figures," to a "case of simple arithmetic." Just as the young pupils are considered to be "little pitchers before him, who were to be filled so full of facts."

A school in perfect harmony with Coketown itself, a factory-city populated by "people equally like one another, who all went in and out at the same hours, with the same sound upon the same pavements, to do the same work, and to whom every day was the same as yesterday and to-morrow, and every year the counterpart of the last and the next." Nothing material or spiritual would have had the right to exist in this community, unless it was recognized as a "fact":

Fact, fact, fact, everywhere in the material aspect of the town; fact, fact, fact, everywhere in the immaterial. The M'Choakumchild school was all fact, and the school of design was all fact, and the relations between master and man were all fact, and everything was fact between the lying-in hospital and the cemetery, and what you couldn't state in figures, or show to be purchaseable in the cheapest market and saleable in the dearest, was not, and never should be, world without end, Amen.

22. Heidegger: it is hard to understand the useless

On more than one occasion, Martin Heidegger tackled the subject of the useful and the useless, especially within the framework of a reflection on the essence of the work of art. I shall restrict myself here to dealing with only one shrewd reflection developed to explain some passages in *Being and Time*. Heidegger worked this out in a meeting with Medard Boss (a Swiss-German psychiatrist who had invited him to hold in his home in Zollikon, near Zurich, a series of seminars on phenomenology for an audience of young psychotherapists): on a vacation spent together in Taormina from 24 April to 4 May 1963, Boss questioned Heidegger on the essence of the human being and on the relationship that the human being sets up with others.

In one part of the conversation—on the *Dasein*, insofar as it is "being-in-the-world, insofar as it is concern [*Besorgen*] for things, and insofar as it is caring for [*Sorgen für*] others, and the being-with [*Mitseiende*] the human beings it encounters"—Heidegger pauses to say something about the usefulness of the useless:

> The most useful thing is the useless thing. But experiencing the useless is extremely hard for modern man. Here, the "useful" is understood as something that can be used practically and immediately for some technical purpose, as something that causes an effect, and as something that allows me to manage and produce. The useful must be seen as something *salvific* [*Heilsame*], in other words, something that reconciles man with himself. In Greek, θεώρια [*theoria*] means *pure rest*, the supreme form of ενέργεια [*energeia*] the noblest way of putting-yourself-to-work regardless of any kind of practical machination [*Machenschaften*]. [It is] letting meaningful presence become presence itself.

Heidegger, in trying to free the notion of utility from an exclusive technical and commercial purpose, expresses clearly the widespread difficulty his contemporaries had in understanding the importance of the useless. For "modern man," in fact, it is more and more complicated to feel an interest in something that does not imply a practical and immediate use for "technical purposes."

23. Uselessness and the essence of life: Zhuang-zi and Kakuzo Okakura

This is an ancient question close to the heart of the wise man Zhuang-zi, who lived in the 4th century BC. In his most important work—which deals with nature, incessant metamorphoses, and the way of life—the Chinese philosopher deals with the subject of uselessness on several occasions. In talking, for example, about the centuries-old life of a tree ("This tree is truly quite useless! That is why it has managed to reach this height. Yes! Divine man is also no more than useless wood") he shows that very often "usefulness is the cause of their misfortune." And, further on, in a very brief exchange with the sophist Hui-zi, we find highlighted the limitations of a humanity that claims to know well what is useful without knowing, instead, the importance of the useless:

> Hui-zi said to Zhuang-zi: "Your words are useless." Zhuang-zi replied: "To know what is useful you must first know what is useless."

In the discovery of the useless, Kakuzo Okakura traces the leap forward that marked the shift from *feritas* to *humanitas*. In *The Book of Tea* (1906), in an impassioned chapter on flowers, he suggests that love poetry had its origin in the very moment when the love of flowers was born:

> The primeval man in offering the first garland to his maiden thereby transcended the brute. He became human in thus rising above the crude necessities of nature. He entered the realm of art when he perceived the subtle use of the useless.

So, thanks to a simple gesture, humanity was able to take the chance to become more human.

24. Eugène Ionesco: the useful is a useless burden

And, conversely, to a bewildered humanity that had lost the sense of life, Eugène Ionesco offered some extraordinary reflections, today more topical than ever. In the course of an address given in February 1961 to an audience of other writers, the great dramatist reaffirmed the extent to which we need irreplaceable uselessness:

> Just watch people hurrying busily through the streets. They seem preoccupied, look neither left nor right, but have their eyes fixed on the ground like dogs. They rush straight ahead, but always without looking where they are going, for they are mechanically covering a well-known route, mapped out in advance. It is exactly the same in all the great cities of the world. Modern, universal man is man in a hurry, he has no time, he is a prisoner of necessity, he does not understand that a thing need have no use; nor does he understand that fundamentally it is the useful thing that can become a useless and overwhelming burden. If one cannot understand the usefulness of the useless and the uselessness of the useful, one cannot understand art; and a country in which art is not understood is a country of slaves and robots, a country of unhappy people who neither laugh nor smile, a country without mind or spirit; where there is no humor, where there is no laughter, there is anger and hatred.

Modern man, who no longer has time to spend on useless things, is condemned to become a soulless machine. A prisoner of necessity, he is no longer able to understand that the useful can change into a "useless and overwhelming burden" and that "if one cannot understand the usefulness of the useless and the uselessness of the useful, one cannot understand art." And so the man who cannot understand art becomes a slave or a robot, he changes into a suffering being, unable to laugh or enjoy. And, at the same time, he can fall an easy prey to mass hysteria (just think, in recent decades, of religious fanaticism) or "some wild collective madness":

> For these busy, anxious people, hurtling toward some goal which is not a human goal or is simply a mirage, may quite suddenly answer some clarion call, respond to the voice of some devil or madman and succumb to some delirious fanaticism, some wild collective madness or other, some hysteria that sweeps the masses. Forms of rhinoceritis of every kind, from left and right, are there to threaten humanity when men have no time to think or collect themselves.

25. Italo Calvino: the gratuitous is revealed to be essential

A shrewd interpreter of the relations between literature and science, Italo Calvino was one of the foremost champions of disinterested knowledge. Calvino, a novelist and essayist, suggested that there is nothing more essential for the human race than those "activities that seem absolutely gratuitous" and inessential:

> Often the commitment that men invest in activities that seem totally gratuitous, with no other aim in mind except enjoyment or the satisfaction of solving a

difficult problem, turns out to be essential in an area that nobody had foreseen and has far-reaching consequences. This is true for poetry and art, just as it is for science and technology.

And, against all utilitarian perspectives, Calvino reminds us that people do not read the classics because they must serve some purpose: they read them solely for the joy of doing so, for the pleasure of making a journey together with them, moved only by the desire to know and to know one another.

26. Emil Cioran and Socrates' flute

In this regard, Emil Cioran—who in *A Short History of Decay* was to devote a brief paragraph to the "foolish obsession with being useful"—says in *Drawn and Quartered* that, as they were preparing the hemlock for him, Socrates was learning a tune on the flute. And when they asked him, "What good will that do you?" he replied impassively: "To know this tune before I die." And in the commentary to his aphorism, Cioran tries to explain the essence of learning:

> If I dare to bring up this reply trivialized by the handbooks, it is because it strikes me as the only serious justification for all desire to know, whether exercised on the very threshold of death or at any other time.

For Cioran, all forms of elevation presuppose the useless: "A useless exception, a model nobody cares about—this is the rank to which you must aspire if you wish to rise in your own esteem."

But—despite the awareness that no literary or artistic creation is linked to a purpose—there is no doubt that, in the winter of conscience we are living through, it is more and more incumbent upon classical studies and scientific research free of any utilitarianism, and all those luxuries held to be useless, to see to the task of nourishing hope, and of transforming their uselessness into an extremely useful instrument for opposing the barbarism of the present day, in a huge storehouse in which to conserve memory and those events unjustly destined for oblivion.

PART TWO

The University as Company, the Student as Client

I have no special talents.
I am only passionately curious.
ALBERT EINSTEIN, *letter to Carl Seelig*

1. The disengagement of the state

Before moving on to read a few passages from some great classics of literature, I should like to dwell briefly on the catastrophic effects that the logic of profit has produced in the world of teaching. In her fine book, *Not for Profit*, Martha Nussbaum provided us with an eloquent portrait of this progressive decay. Over the last decade in most European countries, especially in Italy but with a few exceptions such as Germany, reforms and continual funding cuts have hit schools and universities. In a gradual but very worrying manner, the state has set in motion a process of economic disengagement from the world of education and fundamental research—a process that has determined, in parallel, the "highschoolization" of the universities. This is a Copernican revolution that in the coming years will lead to radical changes in the role of lecturers and the quality of teaching.

Almost all European countries seem oriented toward a lowering of levels of difficulty to make it easier for students to pass exams, in an (illusory) attempt to solve the *fuori corso* problem (those who fail to complete their courses of study within the prescribed time). In order to ensure that students graduate within the times laid down by law and to make learning more *agreeable*, we do not require them to make an extra effort but, on the contrary, we try to tempt them with perversely downsized programs and lessons transformed into a kind of superficial interactive game based on slide projections and multiple choice tests.

But there's more. In Italy, where the *fuori corso* problem has assumed worrying dimensions, the universities that attain the goal of getting students through their course within the legally established time scale are rewarded with ad hoc funding. Those institutions, instead, which fail to respect the ministerial protocols are subject to sanctions. So, if one thousand students matriculate in 2012, one thousand students will have to graduate three years later. This would be a noble and legitimate aspiration if, as well as *quantitas*, legislators were also interested in *qualitas*. Unfortunately, however, owing to the failure to assess the real capabilities that freshly graduated students have acquired by the end of their studies, the existing mechanism changes into a stratagem that drives universities—ever more involved, for lack of money, in the ruthless hunt for funding—to do the impossible in order to churn out graduates.

2. The student as client

As Simon Leys emphasized in a lecture on the decline of the university, students in some Canadian institutions are by now thought of as *clients*. The same result also emerges from a meticulous survey of the functioning of one of the most important private universities in the world. At Harvard, as Emmanuel Jaffelin reported in *Le Monde* of 28 May 2012, relations between teachers and students seem to be substantially based on a kind of *clientelism*: "As fees are very high at Harvard, students do not just expect their teachers to be learned, competent, and valid: they also expect them to be compliant, because the client is king." In other terms: the debts contracted by students in the United States to finance their studies, which amount to more than a trillion dollars, oblige them to be "more in search of income than knowledge."

The money that students pay into the university coffers is of primary importance in the accounts drawn up by administrations. And this datum is beginning to be very important in state universities too, where they try to attract students using all means, including authentic advertising campaigns, just like carmakers and food producers. Universities, unfortunately, sell diplomas and degrees. And they sell them by placing heavy stress on professionalization, offering young people various courses and specializations with the promise of obtaining well-paid jobs immediately.

3. Universities as companies and teachers as bureaucrats

Institutes of higher education have been transformed into companies. Nothing wrong with that, if company logic were limited to cutting out waste and pointing the finger at the cavalier management of public money. But, underlying this new vision, the ideal task of principals and rectors would seem to be that of churning out licentiates and graduates to feed the job market. Stripped of their customary role as teacher and forced to take on that of manager, they are obliged to balance the books in an attempt to ensure that the enterprises they run are competitive.

Even lecturers are changing more and more into modest bureaucrats in the service of the commercial management of the university-companies. They spend their days filling up dossiers, making calculations, producing occasionally useless statistics, trying to balance the books with steadily shrinking budgets, filling out questionnaires, drawing up projects to obtain paltry funds, and interpreting confused and contradictory ministerial circulars. The academic year runs along rapidly to the rhythm of a tireless bureaucratic metronome that governs boards and committees of all kinds (administrative, departmental, degree courses, post graduate) and interminable collective meetings.

It seems that no one worries, as they should, about the quality of research and teaching. Studying (it is often forgotten that a good teacher is above all a tireless *student*) and preparing lessons have by now become a luxury to be debated every day with the university hierarchies. People do not realize that by completely separating research and teaching you end up reducing courses to a superficial and mechanical repetition of what already exists.

Schools and universities cannot be run like companies. Contrary to what the dominant laws of the market and commerce claim to teach us, the essence of cul-

ture is based exclusively on *gratuitousness*: the great tradition of European schools and of ancient institutions
such as the Collège de France (founded by François I
in 1530)—whose importance for European history was
recently underlined by Marc Fumaroli during an impassioned lecture at the Istituto Italiano per gli Studi
Filosofici—reminds us that study is first and foremost
the acquisition of knowledge that, free of all utilitarian
constraints, makes us grow and become more independent. The experience of what is apparently useless and
the acquisition of not immediately quantifiable assets
eventually reveal themselves to be *investments* whose
profits will emerge in the long run.

It would be absurd to cast doubt upon the importance of professional training with regard to the objec-
tives of schools and universities. But can the teacher's
task really be reduced to the training of doctors, engineers, or lawyers? Exclusively favoring the professionalization of students means losing sight of the universal
dimension of the educational function of schooling: no
profession can be practiced in an aware manner if the required technical skills are not subordinated to a broader
cultural education, capable of encouraging teachers to
cultivate their spirit independently and to give their *curiositas* free rein. To have human beings coincide with
their profession would be a very serious error: in any
person there is something essential that goes well beyond their *profession*. Without this pedagogical dimension, very far removed from any form of utilitarianism,
it would be most difficult, for the future, to continue
to imagine responsible citizens, capable of forswear-

ing their own egoism in order to embrace the common good, to express solidarity, to defend tolerance, to claim freedom, to protect nature, or to support justice.

In an intense page from Montesquieu's *My Thoughts* it is possible to find a scale of values that sounds like a necessary invitation to go beyond all restricted perimeters in order to rise more and more toward the infinite spaces of the universal:

> If I knew something that was useful to me, but harmful to my family, I would drive it from my mind. If I knew something useful to my family, but not to my homeland, I would try to forget it. If I knew something useful to my homeland, but harmful to Europe, or useful to Europe but harmful to humankind, I would consider it a crime.

4. Hugo: the crisis can be beaten not by cutting the culture budget but by doubling it

Members of European governments ought to be forced to read a passionate address by Victor Hugo before the Constitutional Assembly. The speech, given on 10 November 1848, seems as if written yesterday. Many of the objections raised by the celebrated French author are absolutely topical to this day. With respect to the ministerial proposal to cut cultural funding, the novelist showed with enormous persuasiveness how that would be a harmful and wholly ineffective decision:

> I say, Sirs, that the proposed reductions in the special budget for the sciences, letters, and the arts are

negative for two reasons. They are insignificant from a financial point of view and harmful from all other standpoints. This is so obvious that I feel embarrassed in presenting the assembly with a proportional sum I have made . . . What would you think, Sirs, of a private individual, with an income of one thousand five hundred francs, who annually set aside for his own intellectual culture . . . the absolutely modest sum of five francs and who, on a day of renewal, decided to save five centimes on his own culture?

This was a ridiculous saving for the state, but one that revealed itself to be lethal for the life of libraries, museums, national archives, conservatories, schools, and many other important institutions. And among these, Hugo cites the Collège de France, the Museum of National History, the School of Paleography, and numerous cultural centers of which France should have been proud. With a stroke of the pen, those cuts would have ended up humiliating the entire nation and, at the same time, the poor families of artists and poets left without any support ("famous artists, poets, and writers work for a lifetime, they work without any thought of getting rich, they die and leave their country much glory with the sole condition that it give their widows and children a crust of bread").

But an even bigger mistake is imposing austerity at the wrong time, when the country needs, conversely, to boost cultural activities and public education:

And what moment is chosen? It is in this, in my opinion, that the grave political error I mentioned earlier lies; what moment is chosen to cast doubt on all institutions at a stroke? The moment in which they are more necessary than ever, the moment in which, instead of limiting them, they ought to be increased and made to grow.

It is precisely when a crisis seizes a nation that it is necessary to double the funds destined for learning and the education of youth, to prevent society from falling into the abyss of ignorance:

What is the great peril represented by the present situation? Ignorance. Ignorance even more than poverty . . . It is in such a situation, faced by such a danger, that we think of attacking, mutilating, and stripping all these institutions, whose precise purpose is to pursue, combat, and destroy ignorance!

For Hugo, it is not enough merely to see to "the illumination of the cities" because "night can fall on the moral world, too." If we think exclusively about material life, who will think to light the "torches for the mind"?:

But I wish ardently, passionately, that there may be bread for the workers and the laborers, who are my brothers; and along with the bread of life I wish they may have the bread of thought, which is also the bread of life. I want to increase the bread of the spirit just like the bread of the body.

It is up to the state education system to tackle the delicate undertaking of distracting people from the wretchedness of utilitarianism and educating them in the love of disinterest and the beautiful ("it is necessary to uplift the spirit of man, turn him toward God, toward conscience, toward the beautiful, the just and the true, toward disinterest and that which is great"). This is an objective that if it is to be attained requires decisions opposite to those made by "previous governments" and the current "finance commission":

> It would be necessary to increase schools, university chairs, libraries, museums, theaters, and bookstores. It would be necessary to increase places of study for children, reading places for adults, all organizations and all institutions in which people meditate, in which they are taught, in which they collect themselves, in which they learn something, in which they become better; in short, it would be necessary to let the light into people's spirit everywhere; because it is on account of the darkness that they lose their way.

Hugo scourges an obtuse, shortsighted political class who, thinking it is saving money, is in reality planning the cultural dissolution of the country, killing off all forms of excellence:

> You have fallen into a ghastly error; you thought you were economizing in financial terms, but what you are doing is economizing on glory.

5. Tocqueville: "easy beauties" and the perils of commercial democracies

In *Democracy in America* (1835–40), Alexis de Tocqueville wrote some extraordinary pages on the risks that may be run by commercial democracies such as the

United States. In this clear and brilliant account of American social and political life, the young French magistrate showed foresight in identifying the risks that threaten societies entirely devoted to earning and profit:

> A great many men have a selfish, mercenary, and industrial taste for the discoveries of the mind, which must not be confused with the disinterested passion that burns in the hearts of a small number; it is one thing to wish to utilize knowledge, and another to wish for pure knowledge.

It is precisely the "absence of the superfluous" and the "constant efforts that everyone" makes to procure well-being that causes the "predominance in the hearts of men of a taste for the useful rather than a love of the beautiful." In a utilitarian society, people end up loving "easy beauties" that do not require effort, or take up too much time ("They love books that are easy to obtain, which can be speedily read, and which require no scholarly investigation to be understood"):

> For spirits thus disposed, every new method that makes for a shorter path to riches, every machine that reduces work, every instrument that diminishes production costs, every discovery that facilitates and increases pleasures, seems to be the most magnificent product of human intelligence. It is mainly from this standpoint that the democratic peoples cultivate, understand, and honor the sciences.

For Tocqueville it seems inevitable that in a "society organized in this way the human spirit is insensibly led to neglect theories." In the United States, in fact, "there is almost no one . . . who devotes himself to the essentially theoretical and abstract part of human knowledge," showing "in this regard, a tendency to be found in all democratic peoples." The race for the useful and the debasement of the activities of the spirit could lead people to slide into barbarism: "While there are peoples who allow civilization to be wrested from their grasp, there are others who trample it beneath their own feet." This is why "nourishing oneself with the works of antiquity" is "a sound rule." Tocqueville does not think, naturally, that the classics and the arts are the only antidote to the desertification of the spirit. But he is convinced that useless and disinterested knowledge can "serve marvelously to counteract our particular flaws" because it "supports us from the part toward which we lean."

6. Herzen: timeless merchants

Despite his dislike of Tocqueville, the great Russian writer Aleksandr Herzen saw in the merchants of his own day a class entirely devoted to trade ("what matters is goods, deals, merchandise, the main thing is *property*"). In *My Past and Thoughts*, he describes with extraordinary effectiveness the gospel that inspires their conduct:

> Earn, increase your income like the sands of the sea, use and misuse your financial and moral capital without going bankrupt and you will reach old age sated and honored, you will give wives to your sons and leave a good memory of yourself.

He who aspires only to "sell goods by putting them in the shop window" and to "buying at half price," ends up "passing off trifles as serious things" and, at the same time, cultivating appearances ("[by choosing to] *seem* rather than *to be*"). In a social context, where people care more for the "exterior" aspect than "interior dignity" it is no surprise if "the crassest ignorance has taken on the appearance of education." And since the useless, namely "all that lies outside trade and the *exploitation* of one's own social situation is not *essential* in bourgeois society, education must be limited." Where life emerges as "a continual struggle for money," man is transformed into a *de facto* "accessory of property":

> Life is reduced to a Stock Exchange ploy, everything is transformed into money-changers' and merchants' shops: the editorial offices of the journals, the electoral committees, the houses [of parliament].

7. Bataille: the limits of utility and the vitality of the superfluous

A pitiless analysis of economics in an anti-utilitarian vein emerges from the pages of Georges Bataille's *The Limit of the Useful*. This work, outlines of which appeared in various versions between 1939 and 1945, was never finished in any definitive form. The chapters that have come down to us, however, contain a series of fragmentary reflections in which two opposing views of the world are compared: one based on the obsessive idea of utility and the other centered on the gift with no prospect of profit. This is a radical opposition

that translates into two antinomic concepts of life: on
the one hand a sacrificed existence in a restricted economy (which allows solely for that which can be used for
production and growth), and on the other hand an existence on the infinite scale of a universe characterized by
lavish expenditure of energy (in which, beyond all limits, it is precisely that which is held to be *unproductive*
that becomes necessary).

In a letter to Jêrome Lindon, in which Bataille explains the publishing project for a new series of books,
the terms of the conflict are summed up with extreme
clarity:

> In my opinion, the general law of life requires that
> in new conditions an organism will produce a sum of
> energy greater than it needs in order to survive. It fol-
> lows from this that the surplus of available energy can
> be employed either for growth or for reproduction,
> otherwise it is wasted. In the sphere of human activ-
> ity the dilemma takes this form: either the most part
> of available resources (in other words, work) is used
> to make new means of production, and we have cap-
> italistic economics (accumulation, increase in wealth),
> or the surplus is wasted without trying to increase the
> potential for production, and we have the economics of
> the festival.

So the different use of the surplus produces two anti-
thetical attitudes that are inevitably reflected by the
notions of humanity and time:

> In the first case, human value depends on productiv-
> ity; in the second, it is connected with the best that art

and poetry can produce, the full flourishing of human life. In the first case, people care only for future time, subordinating the present to it; in the second, it is only the present moment that counts, and life, at least as far and as much as possible, is freed of the servile considerations that dominate a world devoted to increased production.

Aware of the fact that the "two value systems cannot exist in the pure state" because "there is always a minimum of compromise," Bataille nonetheless tries to offer concrete examples, on a historical level, in which *waste* and *surplus* have played an important role in exceeding the limit of the *useful*. In Aztec civilization or in the potlatches practiced by some North American Indian tribes, it is possible to find a culture of the gift (testimony to an economy of dissipation and waste) on which Bataille based his notion of *glorious behaviors*:

> What I have said about the "glorious behaviors" of Mexican merchants leads to the refutation of the utilitarian principles on which this inhuman civilization is based. Basing myself on the analysis of hitherto little-known facts, I shall give a new slant to the history of economics. It will be easy for me to show how "useful behaviors" are, *in themselves*, without value: only our "glorious behaviors" determine human life and assign a value to it.

Now—independently of the criticism that was leveled against the anthropological interpretation of the "glorious behaviors," which for Bataille also included wars and religious sacrificial rites ("I want to show that there is an equivalence between *war*, *ritual sacrifice*, and *mystical life*: it is the same game of 'ecstasy' and 'terrors' in which man merges with the games of the heavens")—it is still interesting to note the effort he makes to identify an anti-utilitarian concept of life in the freely given "gift of itself." Conversely, in a capitalistic context dominated by "extreme indifference" to "the public interest," the "law of expenditure" considers only those "vital movements not subject to any *objective* measurement." But the glorious logic of *surplus* was on the way out when capitalism "required man to give up the waste of festivities" and "other such expenditure" to prevent the disappearance of energies useful for the "development of production" and accumulation. In losing this *surplus*, humanity has lost the values of a civilization in which the gratuitous and the gift contributed to giving life a more human meaning.

In hammering away at the pernicious idea of utility, Bataille also noted down a phrase that, today, could be considered a prophecy: "Those rulers who have only the sense of utility are ruined."

8. Against the professionalizing university: John Henry Newman

John Henry Newman's essays on the university represent a warm defense of the universal value of education. In his *Idea of a University* he challenges the underlying bond, which some would say has priority status, between utility and a university training:

Now this is what some great men are very slow to allow; they insist that Education should be confined to some particular and narrow end, and should issue in some definite work, which can be weighed and measured. They argue as if everything, as well as every person, had its price; and that where there has been a great outlay, they have a right to expect a return in kind. This they call making Education and Instruction "useful," and "Utility" becomes their watchword. With a fundamental principle of this nature, they very naturally go on to ask what there is to show for the expense of a University; what is the real worth in the market of the article called "a Liberal Education" . . .

In Newman's view, the following assumption is false: "that nothing is worth pursuing but what is useful; and that life is not long enough to expend upon interesting, or curious, or brilliant trifles." And the corollary that derives from this is also false: "no education is useful which does not teach us some temporal calling, or some mechanical art, or some physical secret."

Against every commercial concept of education, Newman stresses the importance of knowledge in itself. But this does not mean that the formative path free of professionalizing constraints and the acquisition of knowledge in itself cannot, however, procure a certain *utility*, a series of advantages that the individual can enjoy at the end of a university career:

Now, when I say that Knowledge is, not merely a means to something beyond it, or the preliminary of certain arts into which it naturally resolves, but an end suffi-

cient to rest in and to pursue for its own sake, surely I
am uttering no paradox, for I am stating what is intel-
ligible in itself . . . That further advantages accrue to us
and redound to others by its possession, over and above
what it is in itself, I am very far indeed from denying.

Knowledge in itself, in short, "even though it be
turned to no further account, nor subserve any direct
end," is so good for the development of the spirit of
those who have acquired it that it shows itself to be
beneficial in any case:

A great good will impart great good. If then the intel-
lect is so excellent a portion of us, and its cultivation so
excellent, it is not only beautiful, perfect, admirable,
and noble in itself, but in a true and high sense it must
be useful to the possessor and to all around him; not
useful in any low, mechanical, mercantile sense, but
as diffusing good, or as a blessing, or a gift, or power,
or a treasure, first to the owner, then through him to
the world.

So for Newman—independent of the theological
issues and religious tensions that emerge in his writings—the "general culture of mind" comes before "professional and scientific study," convinced as he was that
"educated men can do what the illiterate cannot."

9. What is the use of dead languages?
John Locke and Antonio Gramsci

How many readers would still be interested in these
impassioned pages of Newman's? Probably not very

many, if we think that the logic of utilitarianism piti-
lessly impacts school and university curricula, too. Why
teach the languages of antiquity in a world where no
one speaks them anymore, and above all, they don't
help you find a job?

Among the lame arguments employed by the new
managers of education, it would seem that—yet again—
legitimacy has been accorded to some of John Locke's
thoughts (even though, to be honest, despite his fero-
cious criticisms, the British philosopher considered
learning Latin to be a necessary part of a gentleman's
education):

> Can there be anything more ridiculous, than that a
> father should waste his own money, and his son's time,
> in setting him to learn the *Roman language*, when at
> the same time he designs him for a trade, wherein he,
> having no use of *Latin*, fails not to forget that little
> which he brought from school, and which it is ten to
> one he abhors for the ill usage it procured him?

With regard to these considerations, dictated by the
most extreme utilitarianism, in today's world people
would smile at Antonio Gramsci's heartfelt invitation
to study Latin and Greek in a striking page from his
Prison Notebooks:

> In the old school the grammatical study of the Latin
> and Greek tongues, together with the study of their
> respective literatures and political histories, was an edu-
> cational principle because the humanistic ideal embod-
> ied by Athens and Rome was widespread throughout
> society, and was an essential element of the nation's life

and culture . . . Individual notions were not learned
for an immediate practical or professional purpose:
the purpose appeared to be disinterested, because the
interest lay in the interior development of the personal-
ity . . . Students did not learn Latin or Greek to be able
to speak them, or to be waiters, interpreters, or writers of business letters. They learned them in order to
get first-hand knowledge of the civilizations of Greece
and Rome, a necessary precondition for modern civilization, in other words they learned them in order to be
themselves and to consciously know themselves.

But—despite numerous appeals and protests in various European countries and the publication of whole
volumes on the defense of the classical languages in
France and Italy, thanks to an enlightened minority
of professors–resistance fighters and intellectual-mil-
itants—no one seems to have the power to halt the
decline anymore. Students are discouraged from em-
barking on courses that will not produce tangible re-
wards and immediate earnings. Little by little, the
growing disaffection for Latin and Greek will lead to
the definitive destruction of a culture that possesses us
and that undeniably fosters our knowledge.

Julien Gracq was right when, in an article published
on 5 February 2000 in *Le Monde des Livres*, he denounced the triumph, in teaching, of communication
that is more and more trivial and based on the progressive imposition of English to the detriment of languages deemed useless, such as Latin:

Apart from their mother tongue, in the past pupils
learned only one language, Latin; not as a dead lan-

guage, but as the incomparable artistic stimulus of a language entirely filtered by a literature. Today, instead, they learn English and they learn it like a successful Esperanto, that is to say the shorter and more convenient route of trivial communication: like a can opener, a universal *passe-partout*. This is a great dividing line that cannot fail to have consequences: it makes you think of the door once invented by Duchamp, which opened onto a room but only by shutting another door.

And if, naturally, thanks to these tendencies only a few students take courses in Latin and Greek, the solution to the problem of teaching costs would seem simple: shut down teaching. The same argument also holds for Sanskrit or any other ancient language.

In some faculties or in some departments, even subjects like philology and paleography are at risk. This means that in the space of a few decades—when the last philologists, the last paleographers, and the last scholars of the languages of the past have all been pensioned off—it will be necessary to close libraries and museums and give up on archaeological digs and the reconstruction of texts and documents. And that will certainly have disastrous consequences for the fate of democracy (as was recently pointed out by Yves Bonnefoy in a passionate defense of Latin and poetry) and liberty (as was stressed by Giorgio Pasquali, who saw in the philological recovery of the authenticity of texts a practice based on the mutual reinforcement of truth and liberty).

At this rate, the end result will be that the slate of memory will be wiped clean to the point of total amnesia. And so the goddess Mnemosyne, the mother of all the arts and all knowledge in Greco-Roman mythology, will be forced to leave the Earth forever. And with her, alas, there will disappear from human life all desire to question the past, to understand the present and to imagine the future. Along with its memory, humankind will completely lose the sense of its own identity and its own history.

10. The planned disappearance of the classics

Within this context, the classics (of philosophy and literature) have an ever more marginal place in schools and universities. Students spend long years in the classrooms of a high school without ever reading in their entirety the great seminal texts of Western culture. They feed above all on digests, anthologies, handbooks, guides, summaries, *exegetical* and *didactic* instruments of all kinds. Instead of dipping directly into Ariosto or Ronsard, Plato or Shakespeare—which would take too much of their time and require them to make an excessive hermeneutic and linguistic effort—they are encouraged to take shortcuts, represented by the numerous anthologies that have flooded the book market.

This infamous educational policy has ended up conditioning in an irreversible manner publishers' programmatic decisions. In Italy the great classics libraries have already been reduced to silence: Laterza's Scrittori d'Italia series (founded by Benedetto Croce), the Classici Mondadori, Letteratura Italiana Ricciardi (which

Treccani has announced it will relaunch) and, for some years now, even the series published by Utet. In France the glorious publishing house Les Belles Lettres is making strenuous efforts to resist but is finding it harder and harder to find contributors able to produce critical editions of Latin and Greek texts. Two other great classics libraries—the Loeb Classical Library and the Oxford Classical Texts—suffer from the same problems. In other European countries publishers often put up strenuous resistance to planned classics editions that are not backed by substantial funding. And all this is happening while secondary literature is increasing beyond all measure.

It is most unlikely that a passion for philosophy or poetry, for the history of art or music, can ever spring from reading didactic materials that, from being mere backup, have ended up definitively replacing the works they deal with: texts, in a nutshell, have become pure pre-texts.

11. The encounter with a classic can change your life

Yet it is not possible to conceive of any form of teaching without the classics. The encounter between a teacher and a student always presupposes a "text" as a point of departure. Without this direct contact, students will find it hard to love philosophy or literature and, at the same time, teachers will not have the chance to fully exploit their qualities in order to arouse passion and enthusiasm in their pupils. The end result will definitively snap the thread that once held together the written word and life, the circle that had enabled young readers to learn from the classics and to listen to the voice of humankind even before life, over time, taught them to better understand the importance of the books that had nurtured them.

Samples of selected passages are not enough. An anthology will never have the power to stimulate reactions that can be brought about solely by reading the complete work. And, in the process of bringing students closer to the classics, the teacher can play a most important role. It suffices to skim through the biographies or autobiographies of great scholars and you will almost always find recollections of an encounter with a teacher who, at high school or university, was decisive in directing their curiosity toward this or that subject. Every one of us has experienced the extent to which an inclination for a specific subject was, very often, triggered by the charisma and skill of a teacher.

Teaching, in fact, always implies a form of seduction. It is an activity that cannot be considered as merely a job, but one that in its noblest form presupposes a genuine vocation. True teachers, in short, take vows. That is why George Steiner did well to remind us that "bad teaching is, almost literally, murderous and, metaphorically, a sin." Second-rate lessons, "pedagogic routine, a style of instruction which is, consciously or not, cynical in its merely utilitarian aims, are ruinous." The authentic encounter between a master and a pupil cannot disregard passion and the love of knowledge. "You don't acquire knowledge," Max Scheler said, quoting Goethe, "if not that of the things you love, and the deeper and more complete that is, the more intense, strong and vibrant that love, that passion, must be." But to get back to our principal theme, in any event passion and love, if truly genuine, presuppose gratuitousness and disinterest: only on these conditions can the encounter with a teacher or a classic really change the life of a student or a reader.

12. Libraries at risk: the sensational case of the Warburg Institute

Corporate logic, unfortunately, can endanger the existence even of major libraries and research institutes of international renown. The library of London's Warburg Institute, just to give one significant example, is one of the most important in the world. Not only for its book holdings (about three hundred and fifty thousand volumes) and for its photo library (about four hundred thousand images) but for the role it has played and still plays in European culture. It suffices to think of the singular nature of this library, whose very structure is reminiscent of that of a book: the location of each individual volume and the thematic organization of the shelves follow a precise logic that reflects an organic view of the various forms of knowledge and their connections, in conformity with the ideas of Aby Warburg and his illustrious friends. A reader looking for a particular book will be surprised to find alongside it a series of other books dealing with analogous or contiguous subjects.

In order to avoid Nazi barbarism, the library was transferred to London in 1934, before it became associated with the University of London in 1944. During the twentieth century the institute in Woburn Square was frequented by some of the most important scholars of the Renaissance: from Ernst Cassirer to Rudolf Wittkower, from Ernst Gombrich to Erwin Panofsky, from Fritz Saxl to Michael Baxandall, from Frances Yates to Edgar Wind, from Paul Oskar Kristeller to Carlo Dionisotto, and from Giovanni Aquilecchia to Anthony Grafton.

But, despite its prestigious history and its immense book holdings, which constitute a *unicum* in Renaissance studies, the life of the library has been in danger for many years: a plan for the unification of the institutes, devised by the university's governors in order to make drastic cuts in running costs, is threatening the independence of the Warburg. Luckily, the indispensable unity of the library and the institute had been stressed by the founder's family in the agreement signed with the University of London authorities. The irony of history: Established thanks to the son of a rich banker who had given up his share of the inheritance in order to obtain the freedom to buy books, the library today is threatened by decisions bound up exclusively with economic convenience (how much income could be generated by a whole building in central London if it was devoted to *productive* activities?). Even though, for the time being, a truce is in force among the opposing parties, the members of the Warburg Institute are not lowering their guard. They are well aware that the battle is not yet over and that the conflict could break out again. Will the library win? Or will the mercenary logic of profit get the upper hand?

Lack of interest in the life of books seems to be rampant everywhere now. During the summer of 2012 in Italy, newspapers and television carried the shocking news that the library of the Istituto Italiano per gli Studi Filosofici, about three hundred thousand volumes, was to be packed up and stored in a warehouse on the outskirts of Naples. As the crates were leaving on the trucks, its president, Gerardo Marotta, denounced the indifference and the apathy of local and regional bodies with regard to the abandonment of a great book holding. Again in Naples, in those same months, dismay and amazement met the news of a theft in the ancient Girolamini library, frequented by Giambattista Vico, from which rare texts and manuscripts of great value were stolen.

Are there still members of governments who can be moved by the words—addressed in a letter of 31 May 1468 to the doge of Venice, Cristoforo Moro—with which Cardinal Bessarione announced the gift of his important library (four hundred eighty-two books in Greek and two hundred sixty-four in Latin) to the city of Venice?

> Books are full of the words of the wise, of the lessons of the ancients, their customs, laws, and religion. They live, they converse, they talk to us, they teach, guide, and console us, and bring near the most remote things, putting them before our eyes. So great is their dignity, their majesty, and their sanctity, that if there were no

books, we would all be coarse and ignorant, with no memory of the past, with no example; we would have no knowledge of matters human and divine; the same urn that holds men's bodies would also erase all memory of them.

13. The disappearance of historic bookstores

Unfortunately, the avalanche of catastrophes does not stop here. The identity of bookstores has also been defaced by mercenary requirements. From being historic meeting places, where it was always possible to find texts and essays of fundamental importance, today they have become showcases for fashionable works, whose success is reminiscent of the proverbial flash in the pan. While, on the one hand, it is impossible to forget the PUF in Paris, near the Sorbonne, or the legendary Divan in Saint-Germain-des-Prés (whose premises, used for decades for other more profitable commercial activities, are now reserved for books once more following the relocation of the La Hune bookstore), on the other hand it is equally impossible to ignore the transformation of bookstores that have gradually eliminated erudition and considerably reduced the presence of the classics (just think of the FNAC chain) in order to give lots of space on the shelves to newly published books bolstered by media hype. The same argument holds for Italy: many historic bookstores are disappearing (think, for example, of the city of Naples, where the closure of the Treves bookstore led to protests) while the big sales chains are pushed into adapting to the logic of the market.

There are few islands of resistance (Vrin, La Compagnie, Les Belles Lettres, and La Procure in Paris, or Tombolini in Rome and Hoepli in Milan) where readers can still find seminal texts almost always. Booksellers themselves, with a few rare exceptions, are no longer the way they once were, able to give readers valuable suggestions for novels or works of nonfiction. Their freedom of choice is now limited to the interests of major distributors who, by imposing their publications in accordance with purely commercial criteria, do not consider quality an essential value. Relieved of responsibility, some booksellers are now mere clerks, whose main task is to sell product in the same spirit as anonymous supermarket employees.

14. The unexpected utility of the useless sciences

This praise for the useful uselessness of literature and philosophy must not deceive anyone. I would like to state clearly—and I do not do so solely to reassure my scientist colleagues—that these pages of mine conceal no intention to bring up yet again the deleterious opposition of the humanities versus science. On the contrary: aware as I am of the distinct roles, I am firmly convinced that science also continues to play an important part in the battle against the laws of the market and profit. It is well known that much scientific work considered to be apparently useless, and not aimed at any precise practical purpose, has later led to an unexpected utility. The inventions of Guglielmo Marconi would not have been conceivable without the research carried out on electromagnetic waves by James Clerk Maxwell and Heinrich Rudolf Hertz: studies, and it is worth stressing this very clearly, that were inspired solely by the need to satisfy a purely theoretical curiosity. It suffices to re-read the extraordinary essay by Abraham Flexner on these topics—and it is no accident that I have included it at the end of this book—to understand that geniuses such as Galileo or Newton cultivated their curiosity without being obsessed by utility or profit. In fact, the fundamental discoveries that have revolutionized the history of humankind are the result, mostly, of research far removed from any utilitarian objective.

In this sector, too, the progressive disengagement of the state is obliging universities and research centers to ask private business and multinationals to provide funding. In any event it is a matter of projects whose end is the creation of a product to be put on the market or used within the company itself. And without wishing to diminish the importance of these contributions to scientific progress, nonetheless we would seem to be very far from the climate of liberty that Flexner talks about with regard to the Institute for Advanced Study, which made some of the great scientific revolutions possible. So-called basic research, once financed by public money, no longer seems to be of any interest at all.

And in light of these developments, can it be accidental that in recent decades "frauds" in scientific research have increased by a good ten times compared to the past? In his recent condemnation of this phenomenon, Arturo Casadevall, a professor at the Albert Einstein College of Medicine in New York, offers figures that sound like an alarm bell: in 2007 alone ninety-six studies out of one million were withdrawn as a result of fraud. This is a worrying statistic if we think that, among the determining factors in this tendency, the conditioning of biomedicine on the part of economic interests plays a significant role. No one has forgotten the famous case of Andrew Wakefield's article against vaccinations, published in 1998 in the *Lancet* and then withdrawn when the author was sentenced for serious conflicts of interests on the scientific and financial level.

15. What do you get from a theorem? From Euclid to Archimedes

That the ancient world was aware of the difference between purely speculative (almost disinterested) science and applied science is borne out not only by Aristotle, but also by well-known anecdotes and biographies of illustrious scientists. Think, for example, of what Stobaeus tells us about Euclid: in order to reply to a question from one of his pupils—who, having learned his first theorem, asked him, "What's in it for me?"—the famous mathematician summoned a slave and ordered him to give the student a coin "since [he] needs to get something from what he learns."

Or you can read again the passages in which Plutarch recalls Archimedes' contempt "for applied mechanics," to such a point that he felt it was rather undignified for a scientist to write about technical issues:

> Archimedes had attained such a refinement and pro-fundity of thought, such a great wealth of scientific knowledge, that he did not wish to leave any writing on that and hence enjoyed great renown and the fame of an intelligence that was not human but divine; holding that an interest in every technology and art that takes account of practical necessities is sordid and servile, he reserved his commitment only for those disciplines in which superiority and beauty have nothing to do with everyday necessity, disciplines not comparable to oth-ers, which give the demonstration the chance to com-pete with the material.

It would be imprudent to take Plutarch's account literally, as many illustrious historians of science have done in the past. Archimedes' interest in so-called me-chanics is evident in various writings of his and, con-cretely, in many celebrated inventions. But, despite this, the portrait of the scientist sketched by the Greek phi-losopher, probably partly conditioned by his platonic convictions, nonetheless bears witness to the fact that the ancients clearly perceived the difference between (disinterested) theory and technology.

16. Poincaré: "science does not study nature" to look for "utility"

Here we shall deal with questions that are developed notably in the reflections of Henri Poincaré. In *The Value of Science* (1904), the great scientist and epistemol-

ogist draws a clear distinction between "inflexible practicians" and "those curious about nature": the former
think only of profit, whereas the latter try to understand in what way we can investigate in order to know
more. The two different attitudes are unequivocally
revealed when this question is put, "What is the use of
mathematics?":

> Without a doubt you have often been asked the use of
> mathematics and whether these delicate constructions,
> entirely the fruit of our mind, are not artificial and
> spring merely from our fancy. I ought to make a dis-
> tinction between those who ask this question: practical
> people ask us solely how to earn money from it. This
> does not merit a reply. It would be more to the point to
> ask them the use of amassing great riches and whether,
> in order to do so, it is worth neglecting the arts and
> sciences, for only they enable us to take pleasure from
> them, *et propter vitam vivendi perdere causas.*

The quotation from a famous hexameter in Juvenal's
Satires—"summum crede ncfas animam praeferre pu-
dori/ *et propter vitam vivendi perdere causas*" ("I hold it
to be the greatest infamy to prefer life to honor/ and for
the love of life to lose the very reason for life itself")—
immediately reveals the criticism leveled by the illustrious epistemologist at those who choose (in a utilitarian
vein) to preserve life in preference to the great values of
life. A life without virtues and principles is no life at all.
(Juvenal's line is found in other contexts from Kant to
Lacan.) So "a science practiced solely in view of its applications" is an "impossible" science, because "truths
are not fertile unless they are bound to one another."

And if "we hold only to those [truths] from which we hope an immediate result will ensue, the intermediate links will be missing and there will no longer be a chain."

But, alongside the "inflexible practicians," Poincaré puts "those who are solely curious about nature and ask us if we are able to let them know it better." Poincaré replies to these people, providing an explanation of the use of mathematics:

> Mathematics has a triple goal. It must provide an instrument for the study of nature. But that is not all: it has a philosophical goal and, I dare say, an esthetic one. It must help the philosopher to delve further into the notions of number, space, and time. And above all its adepts draw from it a pleasure analogous to that given by painting and music.

Mathematicians "admire the delicate harmony of numbers and forms" and "marvel when a new discovery opens up an unexpected perspective." Hence the joy they feel can be identified with esthetic pleasure "even though the senses play no part." For these reasons "mathematics deserves to be cultivated for its own sake and those theories that cannot be applied to physics should be cultivated just like the others." For Poincaré, even "when the physical and the esthetic goals are not united, we should not sacrifice either one or the other."

The analogy between mathematicians and writers is also rendered concrete in the creation of a language: "writers who embellish a language, who treat it like an objet d'art, also make it a more docile instrument, better suited to rendering the shades of thought," like "the analyst, whose pursuit of a purely esthetic goal contributes to the creation of a language better able to satisfy the physicist."

In the introduction to the American edition of *The Value of Science*, Poincaré once more ponders the topic of utility. And he does so by reflecting on the science of the great writer Leo Tolstoy:

> In Tolstoy's opinion the word "utility" clearly does not have the same meaning that is attributed to it by business people, and with them the greater part of our contemporaries. He is but little concerned with the industrial applications, the wonders of electricity or the motor car, which he considers rather as obstacles to moral progress; utility is solely that which can make man better.

If our decisions are determined "only by whim or immediate utility there cannot be 'science for science's sake,' or, consequently, science." Those who work "solely in view of immediate applications would leave nothing behind them."

> You need only open your eyes to realize that all the conquests of industry, which have enriched such a large number of "practicians" would never have come about if only they had existed, and if they had not been preceded by selfless madmen, who died in poverty, who never thought of profit and despite that had a guide other than their fancy alone.

Poincaré offers an example of how the two different attitudes, that of practicians and that of men of science ("selfless madmen"), give rise to two different ways of tackling the same problem; "suppose that we wish to determine a curve by observing some of its points": "the practician, interested only in immediate utility, would limit himself to observing solely those points he needed for some particular end," whereas "the man of science, given that he wishes to study the curve for its own sake, will subdivide in a regular manner the points to be observed, and as soon as he knows some of them he will join them to form a regular graph, and in that way he will obtain the complete curve."

The man of science, in Poincaré's view, not only does not "choose at random the facts he must observe," but above all he does not study nature for utilitarian purposes:

> The man of science does not study nature because this is useful; he studies it because he enjoys it, and he enjoys it because nature is beautiful. If nature were not beautiful, it would not be worth knowing it, nor would it be worth living our life. Naturally, I do not mean the beauty that strikes the senses, the beauty of qualitative appearances; not that I hold such beauty in contempt, far from it, but it has nothing to do with science. Instead I intend to talk about the deeper beauty that springs from the harmonious order of the parts, and may be grasped by pure intelligence. It gives a body, a skeleton so to speak, to the changing appearances that delight our senses, and without this support the beauty of those fleeting dreams would only be imperfect, because they are vague and always ephemeral.

You need to look at "intellectual beauty" which is

"sufficient unto itself." Because it is for its sake, "perhaps more than for the future good of humankind," that "the man of science subjects himself to long and hard labor." Without this painstaking and selfless effort, it would be really difficult to think of becoming better.

17. "Knowledge is an asset that can be transmitted without becoming poor"

In these coming years we need to fight this utilitarian drift not only to save science, schools and universities, but also everything that we call *culture*. We shall have to resist the planned dissolution of teaching, scientific research, the classics and cultural assets. Sabotaging culture and education means sabotaging the future of humankind. Some years ago I chanced to read some simple but very instructive words written on a sign in a library of manuscripts in a remote oasis in the Sahara: "Knowledge is an asset that can be transmitted without becoming poor." Only knowledge—by thrusting into crisis the dominant paradigms of profit—can be shared without impoverishment. In fact, on the contrary, it enriches those who transmit it as well as those who receive it.

PART THREE

Possession Kills: *Dignitas Hominis,* Love, Truth

*It is pleasure, not possession,
which makes us happy.*

MICHEL DE MONTAIGNE, *Essays*

1. The voice of the classics

After this necessary reflection on the useful uselessness of humanistic knowledge, it is now time to give voice directly to the classics, to listen to their words, to let ourselves be inspired by the sparks that can be kindled on reading the works of certain great writers. While today, as we have seen, possession occupies an eminent place in our society's scale of values, some authors have brilliantly shown the illusory impact of possession and its manifold destructive effects on every field of knowledge and all kinds of human relations. "It is pleasure, not possession, which makes us happy" was Montaigne's shrewd suggestion. And to offer only a few additional eloquent examples, I should like to dwell in particular on three topics that, for different reasons, have had and still have extraordinary importance for our lives: *dignitas hominis*, love, and truth. These three domains—in which possession is shown, in and for itself, as a devastating negative force—constitute the ideal terrain where gratuitousness and disinterest can express themselves in the most authentic manner.

2. *Dignitas hominis*: the illusion of wealth and the prostitution of knowledge

Can human dignity really be measured on the basis of wealth possessed? Or is it based on values independent of anything connected with profit or gain? In order to answer these questions I should like to start with a collection of letters attributed to Hippocrates, in which the renowned physician deals with the presumed madness of Democritus. This is an epistolary novel constructed on a paradoxical reversal of roles: the physician, in the course of the account, becomes the patient and the patient becomes the physician. So, in Hippocrates' eyes, Democritus's apparent madness is transformed into wisdom, while the presumed wisdom of the Abderites is seen as madness. The account begins with a significant scene: the great philosopher, from the heights of his house on the hill, will not stop laughing, and his fellow citizens, believing him to be sick, are worried. To cure him, they decide to invite Hippocrates, a physician who disdains wealth and wishes to practice his profession without being conditioned by money:

> Neither nature nor a god would promise me money for coming, so you Abderites must not set constrictions on me either, and let me freely practice a liberal art. Those who ask for payment force their knowledge into slavery . . . The life of men is a wretched thing, the uncontrollable lust for gain sweeps across it like a stormy wind: oh, if only all physicians would unite to cure this malady more serious than madness because men think it a blessing, while it is a sickness and one that engenders evil.

Right from the start, the encounter between these two excellent interlocutors shows itself to be extremely fruitful, especially when they come to discuss the reasons that have caused the philosopher to laugh. This is how Democritus, with extreme clarity, replies to the questions raised by the illustrious physician:

> But I laugh only at men, full of stupidity, devoid of upright actions . . . whose boundless desires bring them to roam to the ends of the earth to penetrate its immense cavities, and to smelt silver and gold. They amass these ceaselessly, taking pains to get more and more, but [as they do so] they grow smaller and smaller. They are not ashamed to be called fortunate because they dig into the depths of the earth with the hands of men in chains: some of these die when the earth collapses upon them, others, after the most lengthy servitude, live in that prison as if in their native land; they seek silver and gold amid dust and detritus, they shift piles of sand, open the veins of the earth to grow rich, and tear mother earth to pieces.

Democritus's reflections do not strike Hippocrates alone but, centuries later, illuminate us readers of the new millennium. To "tear mother earth to pieces" to extract gold and silver, to make human beings die in order to accumulate riches, means prejudicing the future of humanity. It means destroying any form of human dignity. It means being a prey to a dangerous and self-destructive madness.

Above all, wealth and power generate false impressions. This is pointed out eloquently by Seneca in his *Letters to Lucilius*, in which he employs the "all the world's a stage" metaphor. The rich and powerful are as happy as actors playing the role of king on stage may be. When the show is over and the regal attire is taken off, they go back to being who they really are in every-day life:

> None of these men you see in purple robes is happy, any more than you could deem happy those whose roles as tragic actors assign them scepter and chlamys on the stage: first they strut before the public with pompous conceit, their height enhanced by their buskins, then, as soon as they are off stage, they take off the footwear and return to their [true] stature. None of those whom wealth and honors have placed on a higher level is a great man.

This mistake, in Seneca's view, is mainly determined by the fact that we do not value people for what they are but for the clothes they wear and for the adornments they flaunt:

> So when you wish to make an authentic assessment of a man and to know his nature, observe him naked: set aside his assets, set aside his honors and the other deceitful frills of Fortune, strip him even of his body. Consider his personality carefully, what and how much consistency it may have, and if he be great for his own virtues or those of others.

Many centuries afterward, Giovanni Pico della Mirandola, in his famous *Oration on the Dignity of Man*, tells us that the essence of human dignity is based on free will. When God created man, being unable to assign anything specific to him, since by then every other attribute had been given to the other living beings, he decided to leave him undefined, in order to grant him the freedom to choose his own destiny:

The well-defined nature assigned to the other beings is restricted by laws that we have made. You, who are not contained within any limit, will determine your nature on the basis of your free will, into whose care I consign you . . . We have created you as neither a heavenly nor an earthly being, neither mortal nor immortal, in such a way that you, almost your own voluntary sculptor and modeler, may fashion yourself as you choose. You can sink to the level of inferior beings, or brute beasts; or you can, according to the promptings of your soul, be reborn as superior beings, namely divine creatures.

Men, free to inhabit almost any place in the universe, can in this way position themselves on high among the superior beings or down below among the brute beasts. All will depend on their decisions. Those who allow themselves to be guided by philosophical investigation will be able to understand that true *dignitas* cannot be won through those activities that lead exclusively to profit, but through a knowledge "[of the] causes of phenomena, [of the] ways of nature, [of the] ordering principle of the universe, [of the] divine plan, [of the] mysteries of heaven and earth."

And leaving aside the limitations of Pico's anthropocentric and mystic vision, the important thing is his effort to free wisdom and human dignity from the deadly embrace of profit:

We have come to the point, alas, where only those who make the study of wisdom profitable are deemed to be wise: and so it is our lot to see chaste Pallas—who dwells in the world thanks only to divine generosity—cast out, spurned, scorned, with no one to love and protect her unless, by virtually prostituting herself and in exchange for a wretched reward for her deflowered virginity, she puts that sum so dishonestly earned into her lover's cash box.

This is why Leon Battista Alberti wrote a whole book—*The Use and Abuse of Books*—on the need to devote one's life to the study of literature in order to take, far from any logic connected with money, the path of virtue. In the closing pages, which have an autobiographical flavor, the celebrated writer and architect tells us how his efforts were motivated exclusively by his love of knowledge:

> I put up with poverty, hostility, and insults that (as many know) were neither indifferent nor light . . . in a spirit that was whole and strong and noble, precisely because of this passionate love of mine for literature. And this I did, not to attain some pleasure, and not to amass riches, which I certainly would have done had I turned from letters to business . . . The spirit of scholars is lit up by a particular desire not for gold and riches, but for virtue and wisdom.

In the same way, the anonymous author of the treatise *On the Sublime* considered the lust for riches a terrible sickness, capable of corrupting not only the human soul, but also society and civil life:

> The lust for riches, of which all of us are insatiably sick, and the love of pleasure lead us to slavery or rather, send our goods to the bottom along with the entire crew. The love of money is a sickness that withers the soul . . . No matter how much I ponder it, I cannot un-

derstand how we can avoid (given that we hold limit-
less wealth in such esteem, or, to be more blunt, given
that we have deified it) suffering the pernicious consequences of this [sickness] . . . And, moreover, if the
progeny of riches are permitted to breed over time,
they will speedily give birth to those inexorable tyrants
insolence, illegality, and shamelessness.

3. Loving in order to possess
is the death of love

In the realm of reflections on love it is also possible
to find so many examples of the value of gratuitousness that there is an embarrassment of choice. People
who are in love will give themselves for the pure joy
of giving, without expecting anything in exchange.
Real love thus becomes an expression of the meeting of
two human beings who walk freely toward each other.
What unites them is a selfless bond, it is the value of
love itself, able to vanquish all individual interest and
all forms of egoism. And if love is offered as a gift (*the
gift of oneself*), as is pointed out by the wise Berber in
The Citadel by Antoine de Saint-Exupéry, it will involve
no suffering:

> Do not confuse love with the lust for possession, which
> causes the most atrocious suffering. For contrary to
> what is commonly believed, love does not cause suffer-
> ing: what causes it is the urge to possess, which is the
> opposite of love.

But when the desire to possess and the need to dominate the other take hold, then love turns into jealousy.

To love, in this case, no longer means to *give yourself*, but means above all to be *loved by someone* who *belongs* to you. Often, couples behave like animals who mark their territory. In order to possess, they need to *soil*. And, sometimes, according to Michel Serres, even in marriage "property is equivalent to slavery. Again the brand: the ox and the slave are marked with the hot iron, the motor car with the Ford logo, and *the bride with the gold ring*." So—obsessed by the desire to quantify at all costs the strength of fidelity, the exclusivity of the relationship, the purity of passion, the bond of property, and the importance of authority—human beings end up yielding easily to the folly of putting their partners to the test.

To illustrate this danger, I'd like to consider two episodes, narrated in two great classics: the story of Rinaldo and the knight with the golden goblet (as told by Ariosto in the forty-third canto of *Orlando Furioso*) and the "History of the Curious-Impertinent" (a story inserted by Cervantes in the first part of *Don Quixote*).

When night overtakes Rinaldo between Mantua and Ferrara, he finds shelter in a castle. After dinner, the master of the house invites him to attempt the test of the golden goblet. You have to manage to drink the wine in the enchanted goblet: if the wine is not spilled over the drinker's chest it means that his wife is faithful. Rinaldo raises the goblet, and as he brings it to his lips to drink, he puts it back on the table. Torn between the desire to know and a prudent ignorance, he decides not to take the test: the need to know the truth in matters of love can only lead to poisonous suspicions and deadly obsessions. A rational man, Rinaldo senses that it would be self-destructive to seek something one does not wish to find. Because loving means giving up any claim to certainties. Only *belief* helps us to live a relationship based on respect and tolerance: "Until now my faith has served me well, and still does; what can I gain by putting it to the test?"

Stunned by his guest's wisdom, the knight bursts into tears and confesses that he has ruined his love for his wife on account of his jealousy ("So saying the good Rinaldo, and meanwhile/thrusting away the hateful goblet,/saw a great river of tears well up/from the eyes of the lord of that house,/who said, after he had collected himself somewhat:/'My curse on the one who persuaded me/to take the test, alas!/that cost me my sweet wife'"). Tormented by the anguish of betrayal, obsessed by the ideal of losing his woman, he begins to subject her to a series of tests to verify her faithfulness. At first, his wife firmly resists the insidious temptations and the traps he himself has contrived. But when, transformed by a witch into a "young suitor," he offers her some precious gems, his wife, all unaware of the deceit, says she is prepared to spend a night with him in exchange for the gifts: "At first most perturbed,/she blushed, and would not listen;/but on seeing the jewels gleaming like fire,/her stubborn heart was softened:/and she replied with a few, faint words,/remembrance of which is like death to me;/that she would grant me my wish/provided no one ever found out."

And leaving aside the theme of corruption caused yet again by the lust to amass riches—"To what lengths will man's passion for gold not lead him?" Virgil exclaims in the third book of the *Aeneid*—here Ariosto insists on the irresponsibility of the husband, the originator and cause of his wife's betrayal. After having listened to the knight of the golden goblet's dramatic confession, Rinaldo scolds him for his foolhardiness. For Rinaldo, the end of love cannot be ascribed to the wife's infidelity. The real mistake lies exclusively in the husband's mad decision to put his wife's faithfulness to the test and his desire to verify the level of her resistance:

> You should not have attacked her with such fierce weapons,
> if you wished to see a goodly defense.
> Do you not know that, against gold,
> Neither marble nor the hardest steel can resist?
> The fault was more yours for tempting her
> Who was soon to yield.
> If she had put such temptation in your path,
> I wonder how well you would have resisted.

To abandon the notion of possession, and to live with the risk of loss, means accepting the fragility and precariousness of love. It means giving up the illusion of guaranteed, indissoluble bonds of love, and realizing that human relationships, with all the limitations and imperfections that characterize them, cannot be separated from the opacity and the shadowy areas of uncertainty. This is why people who seek total transparency and absolute truth in love end up destroying it, smothering it in a deadly embrace.

It is no accident that Rinaldo's wisdom was to crop up again in the "History of the Curious-Impertinent," from *Don Quixote*. Here Cervantes tells of two close friends, Lothario and Anselmo. The latter marries the beautiful Camilla. And while the young couple are living their happy love story, a nagging doubt begins to gnaw at Anselmo's peace of mind: can a woman who is not exposed to the danger of temptation and who has no occasion to show her honesty be truly considered faithful?

> "Why thank heaven for the goodness of a woman," he said, "if no one invites her to be bad? What does it matter if she is reserved and timorous, if they do not give her the opportunity to loosen up or if she knows her husband is capable of taking her life at the first wrong move? I cannot esteem a woman who is good out of fear or a lack of opportunity as much as she who is able to win the victor's crown in the face of constant prodding and pressing requests!"

So Anselmo, obsessed by jealousy, asks his friend to tempt Camilla to put her fidelity to the test. Lothario resists and uses forceful arguments to dissuade him. In his view, this is a mad enterprise that in any event will not have positive results: because if the wife resists, the husband will not be loved any more than he is already; but if, on the contrary, she gives in to temptation, the husband himself will be the cause of her dishonor. And in the course of this cautionary oration, Lothario falls back on the episode of "prudent Rinaldo" who refused the test narrated in *Orlando Furioso*:

> "[You, Anselmo] will weep constantly, if not tears from the eyes, then tears of blood from the heart, like those

wept by that simple doctor who, as our poet tells us, tried the test of the goblet, the same one that the prudent Rinaldo avoided. Because, although it is a poetic fiction, this story conceals moral secrets worthy of being discovered, understood, and imitated."

This story from *Don Quixote* unfortunately has a tragic outcome: Lothario and Camilla fall in love, Anselmo dies of a broken heart, and the two new lovers also lose their lives. But, before dying, the penitent husband leaves his wife an unfinished message, in which he recognizes that he himself is the cause of his dishonor:

A foolish and unwise desire has stolen my life away. If the news of my death should reach Camilla's ears, let her know that I forgive her, because she was not obliged to work miracles nor should I have required her to do so. And since I myself am the author of my own dishonor, there is no reason to . . .

This story tells us that Cervantes was a keen reader of Ariosto. But the two events narrated in *Orlando Furioso* and *Don Quixote* certainly go beyond the restricted bounds of amorous affairs and interpersonal relationships. They fall within a broader reflection on tolerance. Rinaldo and his interpreter Lothario invite us to relinquish the notion of absolute truth; they invite us to accept the idea that every conquest is always temporary, precarious, and exposed to loss.

Possession, in any case, emerges as one of the worst enemies of love. To circumscribe love, condemning it to live in an eternal prison, will not serve to protect it from the changes and metamorphoses that characterize human affairs. Diderot mentions this, in a brilliant passage from his *Supplement on the Voyage of Bougainville*:

> Nothing would strike you as more senseless than a precept that proscribes the change that is in us, which demands a constancy that cannot exist and violates the nature and freedom of man and woman by binding them forever one to the other; more senseless than a faithfulness that restricts the most capricious of pleasures to a single individual; than an oath of immutability uttered by two beings in flesh and blood, before a heaven that is never the same for an instant, beneath caverns that threaten to collapse, at the foot of a cliff that crumbles into dust, or a tree that splits open, or a rock about to fall?

Love cannot be caged. Love, to use a splendid image employed by Rilke in one of his letters, needs to move freely, it needs an open hand that allows it to linger or to flee, with no obstacles. Closing the fingers in order to block it means turning one's hand into a coffin. Because to possess means to kill:

> Seeing is our most authentic conquest . . . We do not acquire wealth because something lingers and withers in our hands, but by letting everything flow through their grasp as if through the solemn portal of return and homecoming. Our hands must not be a coffin, but a bed in which things sleep the dusk of sleep and make dreams, out of whose depths their dearest and most hidden secrets speak . . . For possession means poverty and anxiety; only having possessed means to possess without fear.

4. The possession of truth is the death of truth

It is but a short step from the theme of love to that of truth. Think of the famous myth of Eros, molded by Plato, which enjoyed extraordinary success above all in the European Renaissance. In the *Symposium*, the philosopher is compared to Eros, because both are condemned to shuttle eternally between opposites. It suffices to read the fable of the conception of Eros as recounted by the priestess Diotima, whose words are reported to us by Socrates, to have a better understanding of the comparison. During the festivities for the birth of Aphrodite, Poros (the god of resourcefulness), drunk on nectar, gives himself to Penia (the goddess of poverty): from their union comes Eros, destined, on account of his parents' opposite qualities, to lose and to acquire all things. Neither mortal nor immortal, neither rich nor poor, Eros plays the role of the *mediator*, symbolically representing the philosopher's condition, forever suspended between ignorance and knowledge. Situated between the gods (who do not seek knowledge because they possess it) and the ignorant (who do not seek it because they think they possess it), the true philosopher, a lover of knowledge, tries to get closer to it by chasing after it for a lifetime.

In his original interpretation of this image of the philosopher's quest, Giordano Bruno takes things to their extreme consequences. In the *Eroici furori* (Heroic Enthusiast), he adapts the classic schemata of love lyrics to his quest for knowledge. Characterized by the unfulfilled desire of a lover who tries to embrace his unattainable beloved, the loving relationship is used to represent the enthusiast's (the *furioso*'s) heroic path toward knowledge. Animated by an inexhaustible passion, this "militancy" thus becomes the expression of an impossibility, a privation, a hunt marked by the elusiveness of the prey. The philosopher, enamored of wisdom, is well aware that his sole vocation is that of pursuing the truth, as Bruno says in *De immenso*:

> In fact, every time we think that there is some truth left to be known and some good to be attained, we always look for another truth and aspire to another good. In short, inquiry and research will not be satisfied by the pursuit of a limited truth and a defined good.

For Bruno, the search for wisdom is a purely human and rational operation. There are no miracles, marvels, magic, abstract mysticism, promises of mysterious unions with divinity or guarantees of another supernatural life: the insatiability of the *furioso* is based on the incommensurable disproportion created between a finite being and an infinite wisdom. But this constant desire to embrace knowledge in its totality can elevate man to know the deepest secrets of nature and enable him to see with the mind's eye, even if only for a moment, the unity in multiplicity. The philosopher's loving service is inscribed within this awareness of an impossible, but continuously sought-for union with infinite wisdom. What matters to Bruno is not embracing infinite wisdom, but rather the line of conduct to be adopted on the path toward wisdom. The essence of *philo-sophia* lies in always keeping alive the love of wisdom. This is why it is more important to run a dignified race than to win the prize:

> Although it may not be possible to win the prize, you must run nonetheless and do your best in what is of such great importance, and resist to the bitter end. Praise is not reserved for the winner only, but also for those who do not die a coward or a poltroon . . . The man who has won the prize is not the only one deserving of honor, but also those who ran well and are judged worthy and sufficient to have merited [honor], even though they did not win.

All true hunters know—as Montaigne says in a fine page of the *Essays*—that the real aim of hunting is the chase and the pursuit of the prey:

> The chase and the hunt [for truth] is our true prey: we cannot be excused if we do this badly and improperly: to fail to seize [the prey] is another matter. For while we are born to seek the truth, its possession is reserved for a greater power . . . The world is none other than a school of inquiry. It matters not who attains the goal, but who runs the best race.

Bruno and Montaigne both lived through the dramatic experience of religious wars. They knew that the conviction of possessing the absolute truth had transformed the various Churches into instruments of violence and terror. They were aware that fanaticism had encouraged the extermination of innocent and defenseless human beings, to the point of introducing destruction and death within families. Yet, as Erasmus pointed out in an impassioned defense of peace, the use of brutality is in stark contrast with the very essence of religion:

> All the books of Christians, be they the Old or the New Testament, do nothing but proclaim the peace and unity of souls: and instead Christians spend their whole lives in warfare.

Erasmus here touches a raw nerve that does not afflict Christians alone. His shrewd reflections could hold good, even today, for other faiths, because the risk of fanaticism lurks in all religions. In every epoch, unfortunately, men have committed massacres, slaughter, and genocide in God's name. In His name they have destroyed artworks of universal importance, they have burned entire libraries with books and manuscripts of inestimable value, and they have burned alive philosophers and scientists who made decisive contributions to the progress of knowledge. It suffices to remember the sacrifice of Giordano Bruno, by the hand of the Roman Inquisition, when he was burned at the stake in Campo de' Fiori on 17 February 1600. Or the horrendous execution of Michael Servetus in Geneva in 1553, on the order of John Calvin, on whose shoulders the accusations courageously made by Sébastien Castellion still weigh. In his *Contre le libelle de Calvin* (Against Calvin's Libel), Castellion wrote:

> You do not demonstrate your faith by burning a man but by having yourself burned for it . . . By killing a man you do not defend a doctrine, you kill a man.

When the citizens of Geneva killed Servetus they did not defend a doctrine: they killed a man.

A terrible paradox: In the name of absolute truth men have inflicted violence passed off as necessary for the good of humanity. Yet again it is up to literature to provide an antidote to fanaticism and intolerance. In fact, even in the realm of matters divine, the possession of absolute truth ends up destroying all religion and all truth. Two great authors bore splendid witness to this when they told the same story in different ways, demonstrating how sometimes a brief page of literature can be more efficacious than a long dissertation. The reference is to the famous tale of the three rings, narrated by Giovanni Boccaccio in the *Decameron* and rewritten four centuries later in the eighteenth century by Gottfried Lessing in his drama *Nathan the Wise*.

In the third story of the first day of the *Decameron*, the renowned Saladin, Sultan of Cairo, summons to court the rich Jew Melchizedek to ask him which of the three religions (Jewish, Christian, or Muslim) is the true one. Melchizedek spots the trap immediately and, like a wise man, answers this extremely difficult question with a story. He tells the tale of a father who leaves, in secret, a gold ring to designate his most deserving heir. And following this tradition every chosen one, from generation to generation, chooses in his turn a son to be honored, until one father finds himself in difficulty because he has raised three obedient sons all of whom he loves equally. How to reward all three with only one ring? He secretly commissions a goldsmith to fashion two perfect copies of the original and, as he lies dying, he gives each son a ring:

> And on finding the three rings so similar that it was impossible to say which was the real one, the question of who was his father's true heir remained in abeyance, and still is. So I say to you, my Lord, of the three laws given by God the Father to the three peoples, of which you ask me: each people believes they have inherited His true laws and commandments, but, like the rings, the one who truly holds them is a question still in abeyance.

The sultan was entirely satisfied with Melchizedek's clever reply, which shows that men cannot solve, with earthly instruments, a problem that only God could solve. Through the original re-elaboration of an already widespread motif, Boccaccio formulates an invitation to reciprocal respect in a spirit of tolerance and civil coexistence. And this difficult but necessary equilibrium was to be relaunched many centuries later by Lessing in one of the masterpieces of German literature, *Nathan the Wise* (1778–79). Once more, it is a Jew who tells us, with greater awareness, the story of the three rings. The three sons, each one claiming the inheritance, go to a judge who advises them to leave things as they are, saying that each should consider the jewel he has inherited to be the genuine one:

> "Each one of you had the ring from his father:
> Each one is sure that his is genuine.
> Your father, perhaps, was no longer disposed
> to tolerate in his house

the tyranny of a single ring. And certainly
he loved all three of you equally.
He did not wish to humiliate two of you
to favor one.—Come on! Try
to imitate his incorruptible love
and without prejudices. May each one vie
to show in the light of day
the virtue of the stone in his ring."

But the impossibility of establishing the true religion
does not prevent people from trying to assess its efficacy, to test its capacity to make converts through a testimony of love, solidarity, and peace.

Religion too, like philosophy, must become a life
choice; it must transform itself into a way of life. So no
religion and no philosophy can ever claim to possess
an absolute truth that holds for all of humankind. Because believing that you possess the one and only truth
means feeling duty bound to impose it, even by force,
for the good of humanity. Dogmatism produces intolerance in every field of knowledge: in ethics, religion,
politics, philosophy, and science, considering your own
truth to be the only possible one means rejecting any
search for truth.

In point of fact, those who are sure they possess the
truth no longer need to seek it, no longer feel the need
for dialogue, to listen to the other, or to tackle diver-
sity in an authentic manner. Only those who love the
truth can seek it constantly. This is why doubt is not the
enemy of truth, but a constant spur to go in search of
it. Only when you really believe in truth, do you know
that the only way to ensure that it will endure is to call

it repeatedly into question. And without the negation of an absolute truth there can be no room for tolerance.

Only the consciousness that we are destined to live in uncertainty, only the humility required to understand that we are fallible, only the awareness that we are exposed to the risk of error can allow us to conceive of a genuine encounter with others, with those who think differently from us. For these reasons, the plurality of opinions, languages, religions, cultures, and peoples must be seen as an immense resource for humanity and not as a dangerous obstacle.

This is why those who deny absolute truth cannot be considered nihilists: standing midway between the dogmatics (who think they possess absolute truth) and the nihilists (who deny the existence of truth), we find those who love the truth so much that they are constantly in search of it. So—accepting the fallibility of knowledge, tackling doubt, living with error—does not mean embracing irrationalism or absolute authority. On the contrary, it means, in the name of pluralism, exercising our right to criticize and feeling the need for dialogue even with those who fight for values different than ours.

In his *Areopagitica*, John Milton, a passionate defender of freedom of the press against all forms of censorship, reminds us that the truth must be considered as a "streaming fountain":

> Well knows he who uses to consider, that our faith and knowledge thrives by exercise, as well as our limbs and complexion. Truth is compared in Scripture to a

streaming fountain; if her waters flow not in a perpetual progression, they sicken into a muddy pool of conformity and tradition.

For Milton, those who rely on "armed justice" with the pretext of defending the truth merely kill it off definitively. And by killing the truth, they end up killing liberty in the same way. Just as, reciprocally, when you kill liberty you end up making the search for truth impossible, as we can see again in *Areopagitica*: "Give me the liberty to know, to utter, and to argue freely according to conscience, above all liberties." It is this freedom to debate that permits man to put together the scattered fragments of truth:

> To be still searching what we know not by what we know, still closing up truth to truth as we find it (for all her body is homogeneal and proportional), this is the golden rule in theology as well as in arithmetic.

There would be much more to say. Far from any possible conclusion, I would like to end provisionally with a fine quotation from Lessing in which, yet again, the emphasis is on the need to search for the truth:

> The value of man does not lie in the truth that someone possesses or presumes to possess, but in the sincere effort made to attain it. For the powers that alone increase human perfectibility do not spring from the possession of truth but from the search for it. Possession makes men immobile, indolent, and proud. If God kept all the truth closed in his right hand and in his left only the ever enduring desire for truth and said to me:

choose! Even at the risk of erring forever and forever I would humbly bend over his left hand and say: Father, give me it! Absolute truth is for you alone.

Lessing's words, like those of the other authors we have discussed in this book, can pluck at our heart-strings, and testify to how the claimed uselessness of the classics can instead reveal itself to be a most useful instrument for reminding us—and future generations, and all those human beings prepared to be inspired—that possession and profit kill, while inquiry, untrammeled by any utilitarianism, can render humankind more free, more tolerant, and more human.

BIBLIOGRAPHY

INTRODUCTION

Pierre Hadot, "La philosophie est-elle un luxe?" in *Exercices spirituels et philosophie antique*, Paris, Albin Michel, 2002.

Stefano Rodotà, *Il diritto di avere diritti*, Rome–Bari, Laterza, 2012.

Jean-Jacques Rousseau, *Discourse on the Arts and Sciences*, 1750.

Denis Diderot, *Satire contre le luxe*, 1767.

Charles Baudelaire, "L'albatros," *Les fleurs du mal*, 1859.

Gustave Flaubert, *The Dictionary of Received Ideas*, 1913.

Friedrich Hölderlin, "Andenken," 1803. On the poetry of Hölderlin, see Martin Heidegger, *Hölderlin: Viaggi in Grecia*, edited by Tommaso Scappini, Milan, Bompiani, 2012.

C. P. Snow, *The Two Cultures*, Cambridge, Cambridge University Press, 1963.

Translator's note: Unless otherwise specified, translations are my own.

Ilya Prigogine and Isabelle Stengers, *La Nouvelle Alliance*, Paris, Gallimard, 1979.

Plato, *Symposium*.

Eugène Ionesco, "An Address Delivered to a Gathering of French and German Writers," in *Notes and Counter Notes*, translated by Donald Watson, New York, Grove Press, 1964.

Kakuzo Okakura, *The Book of Tea*, 1906.

Rainer Maria Rilke, *Letters to a Young Poet*, translated by M. D. Herter Norton, New York and London, W. W. Norton & Company, 2004.

Edmond Rostand, *Cyrano de Bergerac*, 1897.

Eugène Ionesco, "Interview for *Les Cahiers Libres de la Jeunesse*," in *Notes and Counter Notes*.

Pietro Barcellona, *Elogio del discorso inutile: La parola gratuita*, Bari, Dedalo, 2010. In this fine book, Barcellona criticizes those discourses that aimed at gauging efficiency and utility without truly taking into account the conflicts that agitate humankind.

Pierre Lecomte du Noüy, "L'intelligence, les gestes inutiles, le mariage," in *La dignité humaine*, Paris, Fayard, 1967. Also see page 204 of Du Noüy's *L'avenir de l'ésprit*, 1941. Naturally, I have cited Du Noüy only for his remarks on the useless. His religious convictions and philosophical conclusions are completely beyond the scope of this work.

Miguel Benasayag and Gérard Schmit, *Les passions tristes*, Paris, La Découverte, 2003.

Mario Vargas Llosa, *In Praise of Reading and Fiction: The Nobel Lecture*, translated by Edith Grossman, New York, Farrar, Straus and Giroux, 2011.

Oscar Wilde, *Lady Windermere's Fan*, 1892. Also Wilde's 1891 preface to *The Picture of Dorian Gray*.

Voltaire, *Le Mondain*, 1736. It should be said that for Voltaire the superfluous does not only embody art and some libertine values, but also becomes an apology, in an economic vein, for luxury.

For an interesting analysis of the theme of the superfluous in literature and art see the collection of essays published in *Le superflu, chose très nécessaire*, edited by Gaïd Girard, Rennes, Presses Universitaires de Rennes, 2004.

Eugène Ionesco, "An Address Delivered to a Gathering of French and German Writers," in *Notes and Counter Notes*.

On the burning of books and the destruction of entire libraries, see Lucien X. Polastron, *Livres en feu: Histoire de la destruction sans fin des bibliotheques*, Paris, Denoël, 2004; for libraries and the connections between books and liberty see Luciano Canfora, *Libro e libertà*, Rome–Bari, Laterza, 1994.

Benedetto Croce, "La fine della civiltà," in *Filosofia e storiografia*, Naples, Bibliopolis, 2005.

Jorge Luis Borges, "The Wall and the Books," in *Labyrinths*, edited by Donald A. Yates and James E. Irby, New York, New Directions, 1964.

Cicero, *Stoic Paradoxes*.

Pseudo-Longinus, *On the Sublime*.

Giordano Bruno, *De immenso*, 1591.

John Maynard Keynes, "Economic Possibilities for our Grandchildren," in *Essays in Persuasion*, New York, Norton, 1963. For an analysis of these pages published by Keynes in 1930—also in relation to the economist's utopian bent as found in his other works—see Guido Rossi's important reflections in his essay "Possibilità economiche per i nostri nipoti?"

Georges Bataille, *La Limite de l'utile*, in *Œuvres complètes*, Paris, Gallimard, 1976.

George Steiner, foreword to *Nobility of Spirit: A Forgotten Ideal*, by Rob Riemen, New Haven & London, Yale University Press, 2008.

Italo Calvino, *Invisible Cities*, translated by William Weaver, London, Vintage Books, 1997.

Italo Calvino, *Why Read the Classics?* translated by Martin McLaughlin, New York, Vintage Books, 2000.

Rob Riemen, "Culture as Invitation," prologue to *The Idea of Europe*, by George Steiner, New York, Overlook Press, 2015.

PART ONE

Victor Hugo, *Les Misérables*, 1862.

1.

Vincenzo Padula, *Le vocali. Ossia la prima lezione di mio padre*, in *Persone in Calabria*, Manziana (Rome), Vecchiarelli, 1993. Translator's note: In the Italian, the play on words uses the verbs *avere* (to have) and *essere* (to be). The third person singular of avere is "*ha*" (pronounced "a"); the third person singular of essere is "*è*." Thus, ". . . he who *has*, *is*, and he who *has* not, *is* not . . ."

3.

David Foster Wallace, *This is Water*, New York, Little, Brown and Company, 2009.

4.

Gabriel García Márquez, *One Hundred Years of Solitude*, translated by Gregory Rabassa, New York, Harper & Row, 1970.

5.

Dante Alighieri, *Opere Minori: Convivio*, edited by Cesare Vasoli and Domenico De Robertis, Milan–Naples, Ricciardi, 1995.

Petrarch, *Canzoniere*, edited by Marco Santagata, Milan, Mondadori, 1996.

6.

Thomas More, *Utopia*, 1516.

Tommaso Campanella, *La Città del Sole*, edited by Germana Ernst, Milan, Rizzoli, 1996.

Francis Bacon, *New Atlantis*, 1627.

Raymond Trousson, "Le développement de l'utopie moderne," in *Voyages aux pays de nulle part: histoire littéraire de la pensée utopique*, Bruxelles, Université libre de Bruxelles, 1975. Cf. Henri Denis, "Le communisme de More et de Campanella," in *Histoire de la pensée économique*, Paris, PUF, 2008.

7.

Robert Louis Stevenson, *Treasure Island*, 1883.

Geminello Alvi, "Il capitale," in *Il capitalismo: verso l'ideale cinese*, Venice, Marsilio, 2011.

For Stevenson and morality see the subtle reflections of Fernando Savater, "Stevenson e la morale," in *Pirati e altri avventurieri: L'arte di raccontare storie*, Bagno a Ripoli (Florence), Passigli, 2010.

8.

William Shakespeare, *The Merchant of Venice*.

For the literature on Socrates in the Renaissance see Nuccio Ordine, "L'asino come i sileni: le apparenze ingannano," in *La cabala dell'asino: Asinità e conoscenza in Giordano Bruno*, Naples, Liguori, 1996 (but cf., also for the iconography and bibliography, N. Ordine, "L'ermeneutica del Sileno," in *La soglia dell'ombra: Letteratura, filosofia e pittura in Giordano Bruno*, Venice, Marsilio, 2009).

For the theme of the *superfluous*, see Helen Moore, "Superfluity versus Competency in *The Merchant of Venice*," in *Le superflu*, ed. Gaïd Girard. For the equation of the body with money, see John Drakakis, "'*Jew.* Shylock is my name': Speech prefixes in *The Merchant of Venice* as Symptoms of the Early Modern," in *Shakespeare and Modernity: Early Modern to Millennium*, edited by Hugh Grady, London and New York, Routledge, 2000 (see also Chiara Lombardi, *Mondi nuovi a teatro: L'immagine del mondo sulle scene europee di Cinquecento e Seicento: spazi, economia, società*, Milan, Mimesis, 2011).

On the opposition of Christians and non-Christians (considered as beasts and demonic beings), see Michele Stanco, "Il contratto ebraico-cristiano: l'usura, la penale, il processo in *The Merchant of Venice*," in *Il caos ordinato, Tensioni etiche e giustizia poetica in Shakespeare*, Rome, Carocci, 2009.

For Marx's thoughts on Shylock, see Luciano Parinetto, "Marx e Shylock," in L. Parinetto and Livio Sichirollo, *Marx e Shylock: Kant, Hegel, Marx e il mondo ebraico*, Milan, Unicopli, 1982.

Franco Marenco, "Barabas-Shylock: ebrei o cristiani?" in *Il personaggio nelle arti della narrazione*, edited by F. Marenco, Rome, Edizioni di Storia e Letteratura, 2007.

For the Protestant ethic of profit and the English Puritans, see Max Weber, *The Protestant Ethic and the Spirit of Capitalism*, 1905.

For the theme of ambiguity and uncertainty in *The Merchant of Venice*, see Agostino Lombardo's introduction to his Italian translation of the play, Milan, Feltrinelli, 2010.

9.

Aristotle, *Metaphysics*.

10.

Plato, *Theaetetus*.

For the conflict in the *Theaetetus* between philosophical success and lack of success in life see Paul Ricoeur, *Être, essence et substance chez Platon et Aristote: Cours professé à l'Université de Strasbourg en 1953–1954*, Paris, Seuil, 2011.

For the *topos* of Thales who falls down a well causing the laughter of the Thracian woman see Hans Blumenberg, *Il riso della donna di Tracia: Una preistoria della teoria*, Bologna, Il Mulino, 1988.

Plato, *Republic*.

Mario Vegetti, "Il regno filosofico," in his Italian translation of Plato's *Republic*, Naples, Bibliopolis, 2000.

11.

Immanuel Kant, *Critique of Judgment* (1790), translated by James Creed Meredith.

12.

Ovid, *Metamorfosi*, edited by Alessandro Barchiesi, with an introductory essay by Charles Segal, a critical text based on the Oxonian edition by Richard Tarrant, Italian translation by Ludovica Koch, Milan, Mondadori, 2005.

Ovid, *Epistulae ex Ponto* (Letters from the Black Sea), in *Opere. I*, edition with Latin text on the facing page, edited by Paolo Fedeli, Italian translation by Nicola Gardini, Turin, Einaudi, 1999.

In the most recent commentaries to the *Epistulae ex Ponto*, the question of uselessness is barely mentioned: cf. Ovid, *Epistulae ex Ponto: Book 1*, edited with introduction, translation, and commentary by Jan Felix Gaertner, Oxford, Oxford University Press, 2005.

13.

Michel de Montaigne, *Essays*, 1580–88.

The quotation by Fausta Garavini is from the preface to her Italian translation of the essays (Milan, Bompiani, 2012).

Cf. the important work by André Tournon, *"Route par ailleurs": Le "nouveau langage" des Essais*, Paris, Champion, 2006.

14.

Giacomo Leopardi, *Tutte le poesie e tutte le prose*, edited by Lucio Felici and Emanuele Trevi, Rome, Newton & Compton, 1997.

For an analysis of the program of the *Spettatore Fiorentino* and the topic of uselessness, see Gino Tellini, *Leopardi*, Rome, Salerno Editrice, 2001.

15.

Théophile Gautier, preface to *Mademoiselle de Maupin*, introduction by Geneviève Van den Bogaert, Paris, GF-Flammarion, 1966.

For a detailed commentary, see Th. Gautier, *La Préface de "Mademoiselle de Maupin,"* a critical edition by Georges Matoré, Paris, Droz, 1946.

Jean Starobinski, *Portrait de l'artiste en saltimbanque*, Paris, Gallimard, 2004. Starobinski analyzes the metaphors used by the writers themselves to explain the essential traits of their poetics.

Théophile Gautier, *Préface, Albertus ou l'âme et le péché, légende théologique*, Paris, Paulin, 1833.

16.

Charles Baudelaire, *Les Fleurs du mal, Mon coeur mis à nu* et *Fusées*, in *Œuvres complètes*, Paris, Gallimard, 1961.

17.

John Locke, *Some Thoughts Concerning Education*, 1693.

For Locke's criticism of the rhetorical pedagogy of his day see Carlo Augusto Viano, *John Locke*, Turin, Einaudi, 1960. For Locke's concept of the gentleman based on useful knowledge, cf. Ernesto Fagiani, *Nel crepuscolo della probabilità: Ragione ed esperienza nella filosofia sociale di John Locke*, Naples, Bibliopolis, 1983.

18.

Giovanni Boccaccio, *Decameron*.

19.

Federico García Lorca, text included in Pablo Neruda, *Venti poesie d'amore e una canzone disperata*, edited by Giuseppe Bellini, Bagno a Ripoli (Florence), Passigli, 2010.

20.

Miguel de Cervantes, *Don Quixote*, 1605–15.

Francisco Rico's comments are found in his introduction and notes to an Italian translation of *Don Quixote* (Bompiani, 2012).

The comparison between *Don Quixote* and the episode in Tiananmen Square in Beijing was the subject of discussion on the TV show *Le Storie*, broadcast by Italy's Rai 3 network on April 16, 2013. Prompted by presenter Corrado Augias's questions, I reflected on the celebrated image of the young man who with arms opened wide barred the way to the tanks.

21.

Charles Dickens, *Hard Times*, 1854.

22.

Martin Heidegger, *Seminari di Zollikon* (Zollikon Seminars), German edition by Medard Boss, edited by Eugenio Mazzarella and Antonello Giugliano, Naples, Guida, 2000.

23.

Zhaung-zi, edited by Liou Kia-Hway, Milan, Adelphi, 2010.

Kakuzo Okakura, *The Book of Tea*, 1906.

24.

Eugène Ionesco, "An Address Delivered to a Gathering of French and German Writers," in *Notes and Counter Notes*.

25.

Italo Calvino, "The Adventures of Three Clockmakers and Three Automata," in *Collection of Sand*, translated by Martin McLaughlin, Boston and New York, Mariner Books, 2014.

For Calvino's interest in science see Massimo Bucciantini, *Italo Calvino e la scienza*, Rome, Donzelli, 2007.

26.

Emil Cioran, *Précis de décomposition*, "La superbe inutil-ité," in *Œuvres*, Paris, Gallimard, 1979.

Emil Cioran, *Écartèlement*, "Ébauches de vertige," in *Œuvres*.

PART TWO

Albert Einstein, letter to his biographer Carl Seelig, March 11, 1952.

1.

Martha C. Nussbaum, *Not for Profit: Why Democracy Needs the Humanities*, Princeton, Princeton University Press, 2010.

For a defense of humanistic knowledge see also the fine volume of miscellanea *A che serve la Storia? I saperi uman-istici alla prova della modernità*, edited by Piero Bevilacqua, Rome, Donzelli, 2011.

2.

Simon Leys, "The Idea of the University" in *The Hall of Uselessness*, New York, NYRB, 2013. (In the essay at the end of the book and in the first pages of the introduction, Leys offers some interesting reflections on the subject of uselessness.)

3.

Marc Fumaroli, *Le Accademie come beni comuni dell'umanità*, in *Uno scandalo internazionale*, Naples, Istituto Italiano per gli Studi Filosofici, 2012.

For the birth of the Collège de France, see *Les origi-nes du Collège de France: 1500–1560*, edited by M. Fumaroli, Paris, Klincksieck, 1998.

Montesquieu, *Mes Pensées*, in *Œuvres complètes*, Paris, Seuil, 1964.

4.

Victor Hugo, "Question des encouragements aux Lettres et aux Arts," 10 Novembre 1848, in *Actes et Paroles*, Paris, Albin Michel, 1937–40.

5.

Alexis de Tocqueville, *De la démocratie en Amérique* (Democracy in America), Paris, Flammarion, 1981.

Regarding the importance of Tocqueville's reflections against the excessive appeal to utility see various essays by Marc Fumaroli.

6.

Aleksandr Herzen, *Il passato e i pensieri* (My Past and Thoughts), edited by Lia Wainstein, Turin, Einaudi, 1996.

7.

Georges Bataille, *La Limite de l'utile*, in *Œuvres completes*.

Georges Bataille, *Choix de lettres: 1917–1962*, edited by Michel Surya, Paris, Gallimard, 1997.

The quotations are taken from a letter sent by Bataille to Jêrome Lindon on pp. 377–79.

For an analysis of Bataille's position on economics see Giovambattista Vaccaro, "Per un'economia della distruzione," in *Al di là dell'economico: Per una critica filosofica dell'economia*, edited by G. Vaccaro, Milan, Mimesis, 2008.

8.

John Henry Newman, "Discourse V, Knowledge: Its Own End" and "Discourse VII, Knowledge Viewed in

Relation to Professional Skill," in *The Idea of a University*, 1852–58.

9.

John Locke, *Some Thoughts Concerning Education*, 1693.

Antonio Gramsci, *Quaderni del carcere* (Prison Notebooks), vol. III, Quaderno 12, the Istituto Gramsci critical edition edited by Valentino Gerratana, Turin, Einaudi, 1975.

Among the numerous works on the defense of Latin and the classical languages see at least: Wilfried Stroh, *Le latin est mort, vive le latin: Petite histoire d'une grande langue*, Paris, Les Belles Lettres, 2008; *Sans le latin . . .* , edited by Cécilia Suzzoni and Hubert Aupetit, Paris, Mille et Une Nuits, 2012 (this collection of lectures also includes a contribution by Yves Bonnefoy, *Le latin, la démocratie, la poésie*). For the connection between philology and liberty, see Luciano Canfora, *Filologia e libertà*, Milan, Mondadori, 2008 (on Giorgio Pasquali, in particular, pp. 12–13). For the disastrous consequences of a culture that loses its memory of the classical languages, cf. L. Canfora, *Difendere l'insegnamento del latino non è una battaglia di retroguardia*, in the *Corriere della Sera*, 11 June 2012.

11.

George Steiner, *Lessons of the Masters*, Cambridge, Harvard University Press, 2005.

Steiner has written some fundamental pages in defense of the classics and against the invasion of secondary literature: see at least *Real Presences* (1989), *No Passion Spent* (1996), and *The Poetry of Thought* (2011).

Max Scheler, *Amore e conoscenza*, edited by Edoardo Simonotti, Brescia, Morcelliana, 2009.

The quotation is from Goethe's letter to Friedrich Heinrich Jacobi dated 10 May 1812.

12.

Among the many authors who have written about the conflict between the Warburg and the University of London, we mention Anthony Grafton and Jeffrey Hamburger, *Save the Warburg Library!* in *The New York Review of Books*, 30 September 2010 issue; the journal *Common Knowledge* (18.1, Winter 2012) devoted a special issue to the matter, featuring various contributions, including those of the director of the Warburg, Peter Mack, and the Librarian, Jill Kraye.

The affair of the library of the Istituto Italiano per gli Studi Filosofici of Naples was taken up by both the Italian and foreign media. The *Corriere della Sera*, in particular, ran numerous articles about the vicissitudes of the books belonging to the Neapolitan institute (24–31 August and 1, 6, and 10 September 2012).

Cardinal Bessarione's letter is cited in Eugenio Garin, *La cultura del Rinascimento*, Milan, Il Saggiatore, 1988.

14.

For the article published by Arturo Casadevall in the journal *Proceedings of the National Academy of Science*, see the commentary by Eugenia Tognotti, *Scienziati con il vizio della truffa*, in *La Stampa*, 6 October 2012.

15.

Ioannis Stobaei Anthologii libri duo priores qui inscribi solent Eclogae Physicae et Ethicae, vol. II, recensuit Curt Wachsmuth, Berlin, 1884.

Plutarch, "Marcello" (Marcellus), in *Vite* (Lives), vol. IV, edited by Domenico Magnino, Turin, Utet, 1996.

For the controversial interpretation of the anecdote about Euclid and Plutarch's testimony cf. Lucio Russo, *La rivoluzione dimenticata: Il pensiero greco e la scienza moderna*, introduction by Marcello Cini, Milan, Feltrinelli, 2010; but see also Paolo Rossi, *I filosofi e le macchine, 1400 -1700*, Milan, Feltrinelli, 2009.

16.

Henri Poincaré, *La Valeur de la science*, Paris, Flammarion, 1970.

Juvenal, *Satires*.

For a psychoanalytic interpretation of Juvenal's verse in Kant, Claudel, and Lacan see Alenka Zupančič, *Ethics of the Real: Kant and Lacan*, London and New York, Verso, 2000.

Henri Poincaré, *Science et méthode*, Paris, Kimé, 1999.

PART THREE

Michel de Montaigne, *Essays*, 1580–88.

2.

Hippocrates, *Ippocrate e Democrito (Epistole 10–21)*, in *Lettere sulla follia di Democrito*, edited by Amneris Roselli, Naples, Liguori, 1998.

Seneca, *Lettere morali a Lucilio* (Letters to Lucilius), vol. I, edited by Fernando Solinas, introduction by Carlo Carena, Milan, Mondadori, 1995.

Giovanni Pico della Mirandola, *Discorso sulla dignità dell'uomo* (Oration on the Dignity of Man), edited by Francesco Bausi, Parma, Fondazione Bembo/Ugo Guanda Editore, 2003.

Leon Battista Alberti, *De commodis litterarum atque incommodis* (The Use and Abuse of Books), Latin text, Ital-

ian translation, introduction, and notes edited by Giovanni
Farris, Milan, Marzorati, 1971.

Pseudo-Longinus, *On the Sublime*.

3.

Antoine de Saint-Exupéry, *Citadelle*, in *Œuvres complètes*, Paris, Gallimard, 1999.

Michel Serres, *Le Mal propre: polluer pour s'approprier?*
Paris, Le Pommier, 2008.

Ludovico Ariosto, *Orlando furioso*, preface and notes by
Lanfranco Caretti, Turin, Einaudi, 1971.

Virgil, *Aeneid*, books III and IV.

Miguel de Cervantes, *Don Quixote*, 1605–15.

Denis Diderot, *Supplément au voyage de Bougainville*,
1771.

Rainer Maria Rilke, *Poesie. I (1895–1908)*, edited by
Giuliano Baioni, commentary by Andreina Lavagetto,
Turin, Einaudi, 1994 (the quotation is from the letter to
Elena Voronina dated 9 March 1899).

4.

Plato, *Symposium*.

Giordano Bruno, *De immenso*, 1591.

For this passage from *De immenso* and the connection
between the philosophical and the romantic *quête*, see N.
Ordine, *La soglia dell'ombra*, 2009.

Giordano Bruno, *La cena de le Ceneri*, in *Opere italiane*,
critical texts and a philological note by Giovanni Aquilecchia, introduction and general coordination by N. Ordine,
Turin, Utet, 2002.

Michel de Montaigne, *Essays*.

Erasmus of Rotterdam, *Il lamento della pace* [*Querela pacis*], edited by Carlo Carena, Turin, Einaudi, 1990.

Sébastien Castellion, *Contre le libelle de Calvin: Après la mort de Michel Servet*, introduction, French translation, and notes by Étienne Barilier, Carouge-Genève, Éditions Zoé, 1998.

Giovanni Boccaccio, *Decameron*.

Gotthold Ephraim Lessing, *Nathan the Wise*, 1778–79.

John Milton, *Areopagitica*, 1644.

On doubt as an essential instrument for encouraging the search for truth, see the penetrating reflections of Gustavo Zagrebelsky, *Contro l'etica della verità*, Rome–Bari, Laterza, 2009.

With regard to the topic of relativism, Umberto Eco has made several contributions with his customary clarity. Among a variety of contributions, I should like to mention at least *Assoluto e relativo: una storia infinita*, in *La Repubblica* of 10 and 11 July 2007 (it is the text of the lecture given on 9 July during the 2007 Milanesiana festival, conceived and directed by Elisabetta Sgarbi). An important defense of relativism can be found in Giulio Giorello, *Di nessuna chiesa: La libertà del laico*, Milan, Cortina, 2005.

G. E. Lessing, *Eine Duplik*, 1778.

THE USEFULNESS
OF USELESS KNOWLEDGE

Abraham Flexner

Is it not a curious fact that in a world steeped in irrational hatreds which threaten civilization itself, men and women—old and young—detach themselves wholly or partly from the angry current of daily life to devote themselves to the cultivation of beauty, to the extension of knowledge, to the cure of disease, to the amelioration of suffering, just as though fanatics were not simultaneously engaged in spreading pain, ugliness, and suffering? The world has always been a sorry and confused sort of place—yet poets and artists and scientists have ignored the factors that would, if attended to, paralyze them. From a practical point of view, intellectual and spiritual life is, on the surface, a useless form of activity, in which men indulge because they procure for themselves greater satisfactions than are otherwise obtainable. In this paper I shall concern myself with the question of the extent to which the pursuit of these useless satisfactions proves unexpectedly the source from which undreamed-of utility is derived.

We hear it said with tiresome iteration that ours is a materialistic age, the main concern of which should be the wider distribution of material goods and worldly opportunities. The justified outcry of those who through no fault of their own are deprived of opportunity and a fair share of worldly goods therefore diverts an increasing number of students from the studies which their fathers pursued to the equally important and no less urgent study of social, economic, and governmental problems. I have no quarrel with this tendency. The world in which we live is the only world about which our senses can testify. Unless it is made a better world, a fairer world, millions will continue to go to their graves silent, saddened, and embittered. I have myself spent many years pleading that our schools should become more acutely aware of the world in which their pupils and students are destined to pass their lives. Now I sometimes wonder whether that current has not become too strong and whether there would be sufficient opportunity for a full life if the world were emptied of some of the useless things that give it spiritual significance; in other words, whether our conception of what is useful may not have become too narrow to be adequate to the roaming and capricious possibilities of the human spirit.

We may look at this question from two points of view: the scientific and the humanistic or spiritual. Let us take the scientific first. I recall a conversation which I had some years ago with Mr. George Eastman on the subject of use. Mr. Eastman, a wise and gentle far-seeing man, gifted with taste in music and art, had been saying to me that he meant to devote his vast fortune to the promotion of education in useful subjects. I ventured to ask him whom he regarded as the most useful worker in science in the world. He replied instantaneously: "Marconi." I surprised him by saying, "Whatever pleasure we derive from the radio or however wireless and the radio may have added to human life, Marconi's share was practically negligible."

I shall not forget his astonishment on this occasion. He asked me to explain. I replied to him somewhat as follows:

"Mr. Eastman, Marconi was inevitable. The real credit for everything that has been done in the field of wireless belongs, as far as such fundamental credit can be definitely assigned to anyone, to Professor Clerk Maxwell, who in 1865 carried out certain abstruse and remote calculations in the field of magnetism and electricity. Maxwell reproduced his abstract equations in a treatise published in 1873. At the next meeting of the British Association Professor H. J. S. Smith of Oxford declared that 'no mathematician can turn over the pages of these volumes without realizing that they contain a theory which has already added largely to the methods and resources of pure mathematics.' Other discoveries supplemented Maxwell's theoretical work during the next fifteen years. Finally in 1887 and 1888 the scientific problem still remaining—the detection and demonstration of the electromagnetic waves which are the carriers of wireless signals—was solved by Heinrich Hertz, a worker in Helmholtz's laboratory in Berlin. Neither Maxwell nor Hertz had any concern about the utility of their work; no such thought ever entered their minds. They had no practical objective. The inventor in the legal sense was of course Marconi, but what did Marconi invent? Merely the last technical detail, mainly the now obsolete receiving device called coherer, almost universally discarded."

Hertz and Maxwell could invent nothing, but it was their useless theoretical work which was seized upon by a clever technician and which has created new means for communication, utility, and amusement by which men whose merits are relatively slight have obtained fame and earned millions. Who were the useful men? Not Marconi, but Clerk Maxwell and Heinrich Hertz. Hertz and Maxwell were geniuses without thought of use. Marconi was a clever inventor with no thought but use.

The mention of Hertz's name recalled to Mr. Eastman the Hertzian waves, and I suggested that he might ask the physicists of the University of Rochester precisely what Hertz and Maxwell had done; but one thing I said he could be sure of, namely, that they had done their work without thought of use and that throughout the whole history of science most of the really great discoveries which had ultimately proved to be beneficial to mankind had been made by men and women who were driven not by the desire to be useful but merely the desire to satisfy their curiosity.

"Curiosity?" asked Mr. Eastman.

"Yes," I replied, "curiosity, which may or may not eventuate in something useful, is probably the outstanding characteristic of modern thinking. It is not new. It goes back to Galileo, Bacon, and to Sir Isaac Newton, and it must be absolutely unhampered. Institutions of learning should be devoted to the cultivation of curiosity and the less they are deflected by considerations of immediacy of application, the more likely they are to contribute not only to human welfare but to the equally important satisfaction of intellectual interest which may indeed be said to have become the ruling passion of intellectual life in modern times."

II

What is true of Heinrich Hertz working quietly and unnoticed in a corner of Helmholtz's laboratory in the later years of the nineteenth century may be said of scientists and mathematicians the world over for several centuries past. We live in a world that would be helpless without electricity. Called upon to mention a discovery of the most immediate and far-reaching practical use we might well agree upon electricity. But who made the fundamental discoveries out of which the entire electrical development of more than one hundred years has come?

The answer is interesting. Michael Faraday's father was a blacksmith; Michael himself was apprenticed to a bookbinder. In 1812, when he was already twenty-one years of age, a friend took him to the Royal Institution where he heard Sir Humphrey Davy deliver four lectures on chemical subjects. He kept notes and sent a copy of them to Davy. The very next year, 1813, he became an assistant in Davy's laboratory, working on chemical problems. Two years later he accompanied Davy on a trip to the Continent. In 1825, when he was thirty-four years of age, he became Director of the Laboratory of the Royal Institution where he spent fifty-four years of his life.

Faraday's interest soon shifted from chemistry to electricity and magnetism, to which he devoted the rest of his active life. Important but puzzling work in this field had been previously accomplished by Oersted, Ampère, and Wollaston. Faraday cleared away the difficulties which they had left unsolved and by 1841 had succeeded in the task of induction of the electric current. Four years later a second and equally brilliant epoch in his career opened when he discovered the effect of magnetism on polarized light. His earlier discoveries have led to the infinite number of practical applications by means of which electricity has lightened the burdens and increased the opportunities of modern life. His later discoveries have thus far been less prolific of practical results. What difference did this make to Faraday? Not the least. At no period of his unmatched career was he interested in utility. He was absorbed in disentangling the riddles of the universe, at first chemical riddles, in later periods, physical riddles. As far as he cared, the question of utility was never raised. Any suspicion of utility would have restricted his restless curiosity. In the end, utility resulted, but it was never a criterion to which his ceaseless experimentation could be subjected.

In the atmosphere which envelopes the world today it is perhaps timely to emphasize the fact that the part played by science in making war more destructive and more horrible was an unconscious and unintended by-product of scientific activity. Lord Rayleigh, president of the British Association for the Advancement of Science, in a recent address points out in detail how the folly of man, not the intention of the scientists, is responsible for the destructive use of the agents employed in modern warfare. The innocent study of the chemistry of carbon compounds, which has led to infinite beneficial results, showed that the action of nitric acid on substances like benzene, glycerine, cellulose, etc., resulted not only in the beneficent aniline dye industry but in the creation of nitroglycerine, which has uses good and bad. Somewhat later Alfred Nobel, turning to the same subject, showed that by mixing nitroglycerine with other substances, solid explosives which could be safely handled could be produced—among others, dynamite. It is to dynamite that we owe our progress in mining, in the making of such railroad tunnels as those which now pierce the Alps and other mountain ranges; but of course dynamite has been abused by politicians and soldiers. Scientists are, however, no more to blame than they are to blame for an earthquake or a flood. The same thing can be said of poison gas. Pliny was killed by breathing sulphur dioxide in the eruption of Vesuvius almost two thousand years ago. Chlorine was not isolated by scientists for warlike purposes, and the same is true of mustard gas. These substances could be limited to beneficent use, but when the airplane was perfected, men whose hearts were poisoned and whose brains were addled perceived that the airplane, an innocent invention, the result of long disinterested and scientific effort, could be made an instrument of destruction, of which no one had ever dreamed and at which no one had ever deliberately aimed.

In the domain of higher mathematics almost innumerable instances can be cited. For example, the most abstruse mathematical work of the eighteenth and nineteenth centuries was the "Non-Euclidian Geometry." Its inventor, Gauss, though recognized by his contemporaries as a distinguished mathematician, did not dare to publish his work on "Non-Euclidian Geometry" for a quarter of a century. As a matter of fact, the theory of relativity itself with all its infinite practical bearings would have been utterly impossible without the work which Gauss did at Göttingen.

Again, what is known now as "group theory" was an abstract and inapplicable mathematical theory. It was developed by men who were curious and whose curiosity and puttering led them into strange paths; but "group theory" is today the basis of the quantum theory of spectroscopy, which is in daily use by people who have no idea as to how it came about.

The whole calculus of probability was discovered by mathematicians whose real interest was the rationalization of gambling. It has failed of the practical purpose at which they aimed, but it has furnished a scientific basis for all types of insurance, and vast stretches of nineteenth century physics are based upon it.

From a recent number of *Science* I quote the following:

> The stature of Professor Albert Einstein's genius reached new heights when it was disclosed that the learned mathematical physicist developed mathematics fifteen years ago which are now helping to solve the mysteries of the amazing fluidity of helium near the absolute zero of the temperature scale. Before the symposium on intermolecular action of the American Chemical Society Professor F. London, of the University of Paris, now visiting professor at Duke University, credited Professor Einstein with the concept of an "ideal" gas which appeared in papers published in 1924 and 1925.
>
> The Einstein 1925 reports were not about relativity theory, but discussed problems seemingly without any practical significance at the time. They described the degeneracy of an "ideal" gas near the lower limits of the scale of temperature. Because all gases were known to be condensed to liquids at the temperatures in question, scientists rather overlooked the Einstein work of fifteen years ago.
>
> However, the recently discovered behavior of liquid helium has brought the side-tracked Einstein concept to new usefulness. Most liquids increase in viscosity, become stickier and flow less easily, when they become colder. The phrase "colder than molasses in January" is the layman's concept of viscosity and a correct one.
>
> Liquid helium, however, is a baffling exception. At the temperature known as the "delta" point, only 2.19 degrees above zero, liquid helium flows better than it does at higher temperatures and, as a matter

of fact, the liquid helium is about as nebulous as a gas. Added puzzles in its strange behavior include its enormous ability to conduct heat. At the delta point it is about 500 times as effective in this respect as copper at room temperature. Liquid helium, with these and other anomalies, has posed a major mystery for physicists and chemists.

Professor London stated that the interpretation of the behavior of liquid helium can best be explained by considering it as a Bose-Einstein "ideal" gas, by using the mathematics worked out in 1924–25, and by taking over also some of the concepts of the electrical conduction of metals. By simple analogy, the amazing fluidity of liquid helium can be partially explained by picturing the fluidity as something akin to the wandering of electrons in metals to explain electrical conduction.

Let us look in another direction. In the domain of medicine and public health the science of bacteriology has played for half a century the leading role. What is its story? Following the Franco-Prussian War of 1870, the German Government founded the great University of Strasbourg. Its first professor of anatomy was Wilhelm von Waldeyer, subsequently professor of anatomy in Berlin. In his *Reminiscences* he relates that among the students who went with him to Strasbourg during his first semester there was a small, inconspicuous, self-contained youngster of seventeen by name Paul Ehrlich. The usual course in anatomy then consisted of dissection and microscopic examination of tissues. Ehrlich paid little or no attention to dissection, but, as Waldeyer remarks in his *Remimscences*:

I noticed quite early that Ehrlich would work long hours at his desk, completely absorbed in microscopic observation. Moreover, his desk gradually became covered with colored spots of every description. As I saw him sitting at work one day, I went up to him and asked what he was doing with all his rainbow array of colors on his table. Thereupon this young student in his first semester supposedly pursuing the regular course in anatomy looked up at me and blandly remarked, "*Ich probiere.*" This might be freely translated, "I am trying" or "I am just fooling." I replied to him, "Very well. Go on with your fooling." Soon I saw that without any teaching or direction whatsoever on my part I possessed in Ehrlich a student of unusual quality.

Waldeyer wisely left him alone. Ehrlich made his way precariously through the medical curriculum and ultimately procured his degree mainly because it was obvious to his teachers that he had no intention of ever putting his medical degree to practical use. He went subsequently to Breslau where he worked under Professor Cohnheim, the teacher of our own Dr. Welch, founder and maker of the Johns Hopkins Medical School. I do not suppose that the idea of use ever crossed Ehrlich's mind. He was interested. He was curious; he kept on fooling. Of course his fooling was guided by a deep instinct, but it was a purely scientific, not an utilitarian motivation. What resulted? Koch and his associates established a new science, the science of bacteriology. Ehrlich's experiments were now applied by a fellow student, Weigert, to staining bacteria and thereby assisting in their differentiation. Ehrlich himself developed the staining of the blood film with the dyes on which our modern knowledge of the morphology of the blood corpuscles, red and white, is based. Not a day passes but that in thousands of hospitals the world over Ehrlich's technic is employed in the examination of the blood. Thus the apparently aimless fooling in Waldeyer's dissecting room in Strasbourg has become a main factor in the daily practice of medicine.

I shall give one example from industry, one selected at random; for there are scores besides. Professor Berl, of the Carnegie Institute of Technology (Pittsburgh) writes as follows:

> The founder of the modern rayon industry was the French Count Chardonnet. It is known that he used a solution of nitro cotton in ether-alcohol, and that he pressed this viscous solution through capillaries into water which served to coagulate the cellulose nitrate filament. After the coagulation, this filament entered the air and was wound up on bobbins. One day Chardonnet inspected his French factory at Besançon. By an accident the water which should coagulate the cellulose nitrate filament was stopped. The workmen found that the spinning operation went much better without water than with water. This was the birthday of the very important process of dry spinning, which is actually carried out on the greatest scale.

III

I am not for a moment suggesting that everything that goes on in laboratories will ultimately turn to some unexpected practical use or that an ultimate practical use

is its actual justification. Much more am I pleading for
the abolition of the word "use," and for the freeing of
the human spirit. To be sure, we shall thus free some
harmless cranks. To be sure, we shall thus waste some
precious dollars. But what is infinitely more important
is that we shall be striking the shackles off the human
mind and setting it free for the adventures which in our
own day have, on the one hand, taken Hale and Rutherford and Einstein and their peers millions upon millions of miles into the uttermost realms of space and, on
the other, loosed the boundless energy imprisoned in
the atom. What Rutherford and others like Bohr and
Millikan have done out of sheer curiosity in the effort
to understand the construction of the atom has released
forces which may transform human life; but this ultimate and unforeseen and unpredictable practical result is not offered as a justification for Rutherford or
Einstein or Millikan or Bohr or any of their peers. Let
them alone. No educational administrator can possibly
direct the channels in which these or other men shall
work. The waste, I admit again, looks prodigious. It is
not really so. All the waste that could be summed up
in developing the science of bacteriology is as nothing
compared to the advantages which have accrued from
the discoveries of Pasteur, Koch, Ehrlich, Theobald
Smith, and scores of others—advantages that could
never have accrued if the idea of possible use had per-
meated their minds. These great artists—for such are
scientists and bacteriologists—disseminated the spirit
which prevailed in laboratories in which they were sim-
ply following the line of their own natural curiosity.

I am not criticising institutions like schools of engineering or law in which the usefulness motive necessarily predominates. Not infrequently the tables are turned, and practical difficulties encountered in industry or in laboratories stimulate theoretical inquiries which may or may not solve the problems by which they were suggested, but may also open up new vistas, useless at the moment, but pregnant with future achievements, practical and theoretical.

With the rapid accumulation of "useless" or theoretic knowledge a situation has been created in which it has become increasingly possible to attack practical problems in a scientific spirit. Not only inventors, but "pure" scientists have indulged in this sport. I have mentioned Marconi, an inventor, who, while a benefactor to the human race, as a matter of fact merely "picked other men's brains." Edison belongs to the same category. Pasteur was different. He was a great scientist; but he was not averse to attacking practical problems—such as the condition of French grapevines or the problems of beer-brewing—and not only solving the immediate difficulty, but also wresting from the practical problem some far-reaching theoretic conclusion, "useless" at the moment, but likely in some unforeseen manner to be "useful" later. Ehrlich, fundamentally speculative in his curiosity, turned fiercely upon the problem of syphilis and doggedly pursued it until a solution of immediate practical use—the discovery of salvarsan—was found. The discoveries of insulin by Banting for use in diabetes and of liver extract by Minot and Whipple for use in pernicious anemia belong in the same category: both were made by thoroughly scientific men, who realized that much "useless" knowledge had been piled up by men unconcerned with its practical bearings, but that the time was now ripe to raise practical questions in a scientific manner.

Thus it becomes obvious that one must be wary in attributing scientific discovery wholly to any one person. Almost every discovery has a long and precarious history. Someone finds a bit here, another a bit there. A third step succeeds later and thus onward till a genius pieces the bits together and makes the decisive contribution. Science, like the Mississippi, begins in a tiny rivulet in the distant forest. Gradually other streams swell its volume. And the roaring river that bursts the dikes is formed from countless sources.

I cannot deal with this aspect exhaustively, but I may in passing say this: over a period of one or two hundred years the contributions of professional schools to their respective activities will probably be found to lie, not so much in the training of men who may tomorrow become practical engineers or practical lawyers or practical doctors, but rather in the fact that even in the pursuit of strictly practical aims an enormous amount of apparently useless activity goes on. Out of this useless activity there come discoveries which may well prove of infinitely more importance to the human mind and to the human spirit than the accomplishment of the useful ends for which the schools were founded.

The considerations upon which I have touched emphasize—if emphasis were needed—the overwhelming importance of spiritual and intellectual freedom. I have spoken of experimental science; I have spoken of mathematics; but what I say is equally true of music and art and of every other expression of the untrammeled human spirit. The mere fact that they bring satisfaction to an individual soul bent upon its own purification and elevation is all the justification that they need. And in justifying these without any reference whatsoever, implied or actual, to usefulness we justify colleges, universities, and institutes of research. An institution which sets free successive generations of human souls is amply justified whether or not this graduate or that makes a so-called useful contribution to human knowledge. A poem, a symphony, a painting, a mathematical truth, a new scientific fact, all bear in themselves all the justification that universities, colleges, and institutes of research need or require.

The subject which I am discussing has at this moment a peculiar poignancy. In certain large areas—Germany and Italy especially—the effort is now being made to clamp down the freedom of the human spirit. Universities have been so reorganized that they have become tools of those who believe in a special political, economic, or racial creed. Now and then a thoughtless individual in one of the few democracies left in this world will even question the fundamental importance of absolutely untrammeled academic freedom. The real enemy of the human race is not the fearless and irresponsible thinker, be he right or wrong. The real enemy is the man who tries to mold the human spirit so that it will not dare to spread its wings, as its wings were once spread in Italy and Germany, as well as in Great Britain and the United States.

This is not a new idea. It was the idea which animated von Humboldt when, in the hour of Germany's conquest by Napoleon, he conceived and founded the University of Berlin. It is the idea which animated President Gilman in the founding of the Johns Hopkins University, after which every university in this country has sought in greater or less degree to remake itself. It is the idea to which every individual who values his immortal soul will be true whatever the personal consequences to himself. Justification of spiritual freedom goes, however, much farther than originality whether in the realm of science or humanism, for it implies tolerance throughout the range of human dissimilarities. In the face of the history of the human race what can be more silly or ridiculous than likes or dislikes founded upon race or religion? Does humanity want symphonies and paintings and profound scientific truth, or does it want Christian symphonies, Christian paintings, Christian science, or Jewish symphonies, Jewish paintings, Jewish science, or Mohammedan or Egyptian or Japanese or Chinese or American or German or Russian or Communist or Conservative contributions to and expressions of the infinite richness of the human soul?

IV

Among the most striking and immediate consequences of foreign intolerance I may, I think, fairly cite the rapid development of the Institute for Advanced Study, established by Mr. Louis Bamberger and his sister, Mrs. Felix Fuld, at Princeton, New Jersey. The founding of the Institute was suggested in 1930. It was located at Princeton partly because of the founders' attachment to the State of New Jersey, but, in so far as my judgment was concerned, because Princeton had a small graduate school of high quality with which the most intimate cooperation was feasible. To Princeton University the Institute owes a debt that can never be fully appreciated. The work of the Institute with a considerable portion of its personnel began in 1933. On its faculty are eminent American scholars—Veblen, Alexander, and Morse, among the mathematicians; Meritt, Lowe, and Miss Goldman among the humanists; Stewart, Riefler, Warren, Earle, and Mitrany among the publicists and economists. And to these should be added scholars and scientists of equal caliber already assembled in Princeton University, Princeton's library, and its laboratories. But the Institute for Advanced Study is indebted to Hitler for Einstein, Weyl, and von Neumann in mathematics; for Herzfeld and Panofsky in the field of humanistic studies, and for a host of younger men who during the past six years have come under the influence of this distinguished group and are already adding to the strength of American scholarship in every section of the land.

The Institute is, from the standpoint of organization, the simplest and least formal thing imaginable. It consists of three schools—a School of Mathematics, a School of Humanistic Studies, a School of Economics and Politics. Each school is made up of a permanent group of professors and an annually changing group of members. Each school manages its own affairs as it pleases; within each group each individual disposes of his time and energy as he pleases. The members who already have come from twenty-two foreign countries and thirty-nine institutions of higher learning in the United States are admitted, if deemed worthy, by the several groups. They enjoy precisely the same freedom as the professors. They may work with this or that professor, as they severally arrange; they may work alone, consulting from time to time anyone likely to be helpful. No routine is followed; no lines are drawn between professors, members, or visitors. Princeton students and professors and Institute members and professors mingle so freely as to be indistinguishable. Learning as such is cultivated. The results to the individual and to society are left to take care of themselves. No faculty meetings are held; no committees exist. Thus men with ideas enjoy conditions favorable to reflection and to conference. A mathematician may cultivate mathematics without distraction; so may a humanist in his field, an economist or a student of politics in his. Administration has been minimized in extent and importance. Men without ideas, without power of concentration on ideas, would not be at home in the Institute.

I can perhaps make this point clearer by citing briefly a few illustrations. A stipend was awarded to enable a Harvard professor to come to Princeton: he wrote asking,

"What are my duties?"

I replied: "You have no duties—only opportunities."

An able young mathematician, having spent a year at Princeton, came to bid me good-by. As he was about to leave, he remarked:

"Perhaps you would like to know what this year has meant to me."

"Yes," I answered.

"Mathematics," he rejoined, "is developing rapidly; the current literature is extensive. It is now over ten years since I took my Ph.D. degree. For a while I could keep up with my subject; but latterly that has become increasingly difficult and uncertain. Now, after a year here, the blinds are raised; the room is light; the windows are open. I have in my head two papers that I shall shortly write."

"How long will this last?" I asked.

"Five years, perhaps ten."

"Then what?"

"I shall come back."

A third example is of recent occurrence. A professor in a large Western university arrived in Princeton at the end of last December. He had in mind to resume some work with Professor Morey (at Princeton University). But Morey suggested that he might find it worthwhile to see Panofsky and Swarzenski (at the Institute). Now he is busy with all three.

"I shall stay," he added, "until next October."

"You will find it hot in midsummer," I said.

"I shall be too busy and too happy to notice it."

Thus freedom brings not stagnation, but rather the danger of overwork. The wife of an English member recently asked:

"Does everyone work until two o'clock in the morning?"

The Institute has had thus far no building. At this moment the mathematicians are guests of the Princeton mathematicians in Fine Hall; some of the humanists are guests of the Princeton humanists in McCormick Hall; others work in rooms scattered through the town. The economists now occupy a suite at The Princeton Inn. My own quarters are located in an office building on Nassau Street, where I work among shopkeepers, dentists, lawyers, chiropractors, and groups of Princeton scholars conducting a local government survey and a study of population. Bricks and mortar are thus quite inessential, as President Gilman proved in Baltimore sixty-odd years ago. Nevertheless, we miss informal contact with one another and are about to remedy this defect by the erection of a building provided by the founders, to be called Fuld Hall. But formality shall go no farther. The Institute must remain small; and it will hold fast to the conviction that The Institute Group desires leisure, security, freedom from organization and routine, and, finally, informal contacts with the scholars of Princeton University and others who from time to time can be lured to Princeton from distant places. Among these Niels Bohr has come from Copenhagen, von Laue from Berlin, Levi Civita from Rome, André Weil from Strasbourg, Dirac and G. H. Hardy from Cambridge, Pauli from Zurich, Lemaitre from Louvain, Wade-Gery from Oxford, and Americans from Harvard, Yale, Columbia, Cornell, Johns Hopkins, Chicago, California, and other centers of light and learning.

We make ourselves no promises, but we cherish the hope that the unobstructed pursuit of useless knowledge will prove to have consequences in the future as in the past. Not for a moment, however, do we defend the Institute on that ground. It exists as a paradise for scholars who, like poets and musicians, have won the right to do as they please and who accomplish most when enabled to do so.